Excel 2000

For Windows®

FOR DUMMIES®

QUICK REFERENCE

by John Walkenbach

Wiley Publishing, Inc.

Excel 2000 For Windows® For Dummies® Quick Reference

Published by
Wiley Publishing, Inc.
909 Third Avenue
New York, NY 10022
www.hungryminds.com

For general information on our other products and services or to obtain technical support, please contact our Customer Care Department within the U.S. at 800-762-2974, outside the U.S. at 317-572-3993, or fax 317-572-4002.

Wiley also publishes its books in a variety of electronic formats. Some content that appears in print may not be available in electronic books.

Library of Congress Cataloging-in-Publication Data:
Library of Congress Catalog Card No.: 99-60739

ISBN: 0-7645-0447-9

Printed in the United States of America

20 19 18 17 16 15 14 13 12

About the Author

John Walkenbach has been involved with computers for the past 25 years. He has written more than 250 articles and reviews for publications such as *PC World, Windows, PC/Computing,* and *InfoWorld.* In addition, he's the best-selling author of more than a dozen books, including the *Excel 97 For Windows Bible, Excel For Windows 95 Power Programming With VBA,* and *Excel Programming For Windows 95 For Dummies.* John holds a Ph.D. in experimental psychology from the University of Montana, and has worked as an instructor, consultant, programmer, and market research manager for the largest S&L ever to fail (and he takes no responsibility for that). Currently, he heads JWalk and Associates, a small consulting firm in southern California. John also maintains "The Spreadsheet Page" on the World Wide Web (http://www.j-walk.com/ss). In his spare time, he likes to annoy his neighbors with loud blues guitar playing and weird sounds from his synthesizers.

Dedication

This book is dedicated to VaRene, Dustin, Marisa, and K.C.

Author's Acknowledgments

Thanks to all the folks at IDG Books who helped with the update of this book. There's not room to acknowledge them all, so I'd like to thank a few people who played a major role in the process. Bill Helling, my project editor, did a wonderful job coordinating the entire effort. Thanks also to Billie Williams, my main copy editor, whose excellent work helped make this book much more readable. I'm also indebted to Jim McCarter, who provided a thorough technical review and made some great suggestions for improvement.

John Walkenbach

La Jolla, California

Publisher's Acknowledgments

We're proud of this book; please register your comments through our online registration form located at: www.dummies.com/register.

Some of the people who helped bring this book to market include the following:

Acquisitions, Editorial, and Media Development

Project Editor: Bill Helling

Acquisitions Editor: Steve Hayes

Copy Editor: Billie Williams

Technical Editor: Jim McCarter

Associate Permissions Editor: Carmen Krikorian

Editorial Manager: Kelly Ewing

Media Development Manager: Heather Heath Dismore

Editorial Assistant: Paul E. Kuzmic

Production

Project Coordinator: Regina Snyder

Associate Project Coordinator: Maridee V. Ennis

Layout and Graphics: Angela F. Hunckler, Jane E. Martin, Brent Savage, Jacque Schneider, Anne Sipahimalani, Brian Torwelle

Proofreaders: Kelli Botta, Joel K. Draper Rebecca Senninger, Ethel M. Winslow, Janet M. Withers

Indexer: Sherry Massey

General and Administrative

Wiley Technology Publishing Group: Richard Swadley, Vice President and Executive Group Publisher; Bob Ipsen, Vice President and Group Publisher; Joseph Wikert, Vice President and Publisher; Barry Pruett, Vice President and Publisher; Mary Bednarek, Editorial Director; Mary C. Corder, Editorial Director; Andy Cummings, Editorial Director

Wiley Manufacturing: Ivor Parker, Vice President, Manufacturing

Wiley Marketing: John Helmus, Assistant Vice President, Director of Marketing

Wiley Composition Services for Branded Press: Debbie Stailey, Production Director

Table of Contents

Part IV: Entering and Editing Worksheet Data 77

How to Use This Book

Greetings. You're holding in your hands one of a different breed of computer reference books — a book written for normal people (not computer geeks). The *Excel 2000 For Windows For Dummies Quick Reference* is for those of you who have no aspirations of becoming a spreadsheet wizard. Rather, you want to be able to do your job efficiently so that you can move on to more important things — like having a life.

This Book: Who Needs It?

I wrote this book for the hundreds of thousands of beginning to intermediate Microsoft Excel 2000 users who have better things to do with their time than wade through technical drivel just to figure out how to do something so they can go home.

Excel can be used at many different levels, and it's a safe bet that the majority of Excel users don't really have a clue as to what the program can really do when all the stops are pulled out. My goal is to open the door to some of the cool things that Excel can do — and do so in a way that doesn't put you to sleep.

On the one hand, Excel is very easy to use. I can spend 20 minutes with a new user and have them doing semi-useful things by themselves afterward. But practically all Excel users eventually reach a head-scratching point when they want to do something, but can't figure out how. This book comes to the rescue.

The truth of the matter is that virtually no one actually needs or uses all of the Excel commands. Most users get by just fine after they learn the basics. But if you stick to the basics, you run the risk of causing more work for yourself. For example, Excel has commands that automate things that may take you an hour to do manually. Saving ten minutes here or half an hour there adds up. You'll have more time for fun things and can maybe even get out of the office at a reasonable hour — not to mention the fact that people will be amazed at how efficient you've become.

Ways to use this book

This book is organized into several parts. Topics in each part are alphabetized by task, and each task is designed as a self-contained unit. In other words, the book is intended to minimize the amount of reading you have to do.

You can use this book in several ways:

✦ If you need to find out how to do something in Excel, look up the general topic in the Table of Contents and see if it sounds like what you want to accomplish. If so, turn to that part and find the appropriate section.

✦ If you don't even have a clue as to the proper command to look up, head for the index and look at words that describe what you want to do. This usually steers you to the section that you're looking for.

✦ If you come across a term you're unfamiliar with, look it up in this book's glossary, aptly named "Techie Talk." I've thrown in lots of juicy definitions to help you out.

✦ If you find yourself with a spare hour or two while circling over your favorite busy airport waiting to land, browse through this book and read things that are interesting to you. You just may discover something that you didn't know Excel could do — and it's just what you need for a project you're working on.

✦ Keep this book lying around on your desk. That way, people will come by and make some sort of comment about the title of the book. This will inevitably lead to disparaging remarks about your intelligence level. The ensuing conversation is a good way to kill some time when you should be working.

How not to use this book

Whatever you do, don't read this book from cover to cover. Frankly, the plot stinks, the character development leaves much to be desired, and you'll be disappointed by the ending. Although it's moderately entertaining, the book is not exactly what you would call a page-turner.

What the Little Pictures Mean

All the good computer books have little icons sprinkled liberally throughout their pages. These icons work great for visually oriented people and tell you in an instant a few key things about each command. Here's what the icons in this book mean:

This icon flags a command that is available only if you've loaded a particular add-in file.

This icon signals the fastest and most efficient way to perform a task. Often, the fastest way is to use a toolbar button. In that case, you just see the button in the margin instead of this icon.

This icon flags problem areas that can mess up your work if you're not on your toes.

This icon flags a way of using the command that may not be immediately obvious to the average bear.

This icon indicates a feature that is available only in Excel 2000.

This icon tells you where to go if you require additional information.

This icon points out a feature that works with Microsoft's Intellimouse.

Important Note: This book covers Excel 2000 for Windows. Most of the book is also relevant to Excel 97 and Excel 95, but the latest version has several new features, which I point out in the text.

Part 1

Getting to Know Excel 2000

Microsoft Excel 2000 is one of several spreadsheet programs that are available. Others that you may have heard of include Lotus 1-2-3 and Corel Quattro Pro. Many others have come and gone over the years, but these are by far the most popular ones.

In this part . . .

✓ **Discovering cells and ranges**

✓ **Checking out the Excel screen**

✓ **Getting acquainted with the Office Assistant**

✓ **Using boxes and toolbars**

Excel behind the Scenes

A *spreadsheet program* is essentially a highly interactive environment that lets you work with numbers and text in a large grid of cells. Excel also creates graphs and maps from numbers stored in a worksheet and works with database information stored in a record and field format.

Excel files are known as *workbooks*. A single workbook can store as many sheets as will fit into memory, and these sheets are stacked like the pages in a notebook. Sheets can be either *worksheets* (a normal spreadsheet-type sheet) or *chart sheets* (a special sheet that holds a single chart).

Most of the time, you work with worksheets — each of which has exactly 65,536 rows and 256 columns. Rows are numbered from 1 to 65,536, and columns are labeled with letters. Column 1 is A, column 26 is Z, column 27 is AA, column 52 is AZ, column 53 is BA, and so on, up to column 256 (which is IV — not Roman numeral 4!).

The intersection of a row and column is called a *cell*. A quick calculation with Excel tells me that this works out to 16,777,216 cells — which should be enough for most people. Cells have *addresses,* which are based on the row and column that they are in. The upper-left cell in a worksheet is called A1, and the cell way down at the bottom is called IV65536. Cell K9 (also known as the dog cell) is the intersection of the eleventh column and the ninth row.

A cell in Excel can hold a number, some text, a formula, or nothing at all. You already know what numbers and text are, but you may be a bit fuzzy on the concept of a formula. A *formula* is a special way to tell Excel to perform a calculation using information stored in other cells. For example, you can insert a formula that tells Excel to add up the values in the first 10 cells in column A and to display the result in the cell that contains the formula.

Formulas can use normal arithmetic operators such as + (plus), – (minus), * (multiply), and / (divide). They can also use special built-in functions that let you do powerful things without much effort on your part. For example, Excel has functions that add up a range of values, calculate square roots, compute loan payments, and even tell you the time of day. Part V covers how to use the various functions of Excel.

When you create a chart from numbers stored in a worksheet, you can put the chart directly on the worksheet or in a special chart sheet in the workbook. When you're working with a chart, some of Excel's menus change so that they are appropriate for chart-type operations.

If your worksheet contains geographic data, you can create maps from the data. Maps reside on a worksheet (there's no such thing as a map sheet).

The active cell and ranges

In Excel, one of the cells in a worksheet is always the *active cell*. The active cell is the one that's selected, and it is displayed with a thicker border. Its contents appear in the *formula bar.* You can also select a group (or range) of cells by clicking and dragging the mouse over them. When you issue a command that does something to a cell or a range of cells, that something will be done to the active cell or to the selected range of cells.

The selected *range* is usually a group of contiguous cells, but it doesn't have to be. If you hold down the Ctrl key while you click and drag the mouse, you can select more than one group of cells.

Navigational techniques

With more than 16 million cells in a worksheet, you need ways to move to specific cells. Fortunately, Excel provides you with many techniques to move around a worksheet. As always, you can use either your mouse or the keyboard on your navigational journeys. The following table lists the keystrokes that allow you to move through a worksheet.

Keys	Action
Up arrow	Moves the active cell up one row
Down arrow	Moves the active cell down one row
Left arrow	Moves the active cell one column to the left
Right arrow	Moves the active cell one column to the right
PgUp	Moves the active cell up one screen
PgDn	Moves the active cell down one screen
Alt+PgDn	Moves the active cell right one screen
Alt+PgUp	Moves the active cell left one screen
Ctrl+Backspace	Scrolls to display the active cell
Up arrow*	Scrolls the screen up one row (active cell does not change)
Down arrow*	Scrolls the screen down one row (active cell does not change)
Left arrow*	Scrolls the screen left one column (active cell does not change)
Right arrow*	Scrolls the screen right one column (active cell does not change)

* With Scroll Lock on

The actions for some of the keys in the preceding table may be different, depending on the transition options you've set. Select the Tools⇔Options command and then click the Transition tab in the Options dialog box. If the Transition Navigation Keys option is checked, the navigation keys correspond to those used in older versions of Lotus 1-2-3. Generally, it's better to use the standard Excel navigation keys than those for 1-2-3.

Acquainting Yourself with the Excel Screen

The following figure shows a typical Excel screen, with some of the important parts pointed out. This terminology rears its ugly head throughout this book, so pay attention.

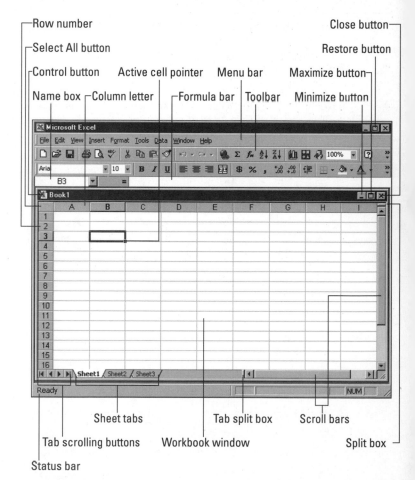

Introducing the Office Assistant

Excel comes with an interactive help tool called the Office Assistant. The Office Assistant takes the form of an animated character (you can choose from eight characters) that floats over the Excel screen.

 If the Office Assistant is not visible, click the Microsoft Excel Help button in the Standard toolbar. You can drag the assistant to any location on the screen.

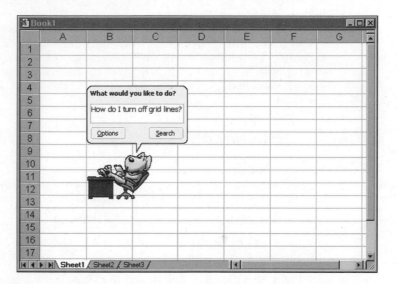

The Office Assistant provides the following types of help:

+ It displays a tip of the day when you start Excel (optional).

+ It watches you work and lets you know when there's a more efficient way to perform an operation. A yellow light bulb appears next to the Assistant (or in the Microsoft Excel Help button) when it has a tip for you. Click the light bulb to read the tip.

+ It provides automatic help with certain tasks. For example, if you're about to create a chart, the Assistant asks if you need help.

+ It responds to natural language questions. Just type your question in the Assistant's box and click Search.

If you find that the Office Assistant is sometimes too helpful and it gets distracting, customize it to your liking: Right-click the Assistant and choose Options from the shortcut menu. The Office Assistant dialog box appears with the Options tab selected.

A new feature in the Options tab allows you the turn the Assistant on and off. To turn the Assistant off, clear the checkbox next to the Use the Office Assistant label. To turn the Assistant on, select the Help⇨Show the Office Assistant command.

Remember: You can select Help⇨Hide the Office Assistant to hide the Assistant when the Assistant is turned on. Hiding the Assistant is not the same as turning the Assistant off. Hiding the Assistant simply hides the icon from view. If you later click the Microsoft Excel Help button on the toolbar, the Assistant reappears. When you turn the Assistant off and then click the Microsoft Excel Help button, Excel displays the Help dialog box but does not show the Assistant.

Using Excel Commands

Excel has many commands that you use to do the things that spreadsheet users do. Here's a typical Excel command: File⇨Open. Use this command to open a workbook file so you can work in it.

You can invoke this command in several different ways:

✦ Click the File menu on the menu bar with the mouse and then click the Open command.

✦ Press Alt+F (for File) and then O (for Open).

✦ Press Alt or F10 to activate the menu bar; then use the arrow keys to move to the File menu. Press Enter and move to the Open command using the arrow keys. Press Enter again to issue the command.

✦ Click the button on the Standard toolbar that looks like a file folder opening up.

✦ Press Ctrl+F12 (or Ctrl+Alt+F2 if your keyboard lacks an F12 function key).

All of these techniques have the same result: The Open dialog box pops up. This dialog box lets you tell Excel which file you want to open. Once the dialog box displays, you can use your mouse or keyboard to carry on the dialog and tell Excel what you're trying to do.

While having all of these command options available may seem a bit confusing, you certainly don't have to know them all. Most people simply choose one method and stick to it. Also, not all commands have so many options. Because opening files is done so frequently, Excel designers went overboard and came up with several ways to do it.

Most commands lead to a dialog box, but some commands do their thing immediately with no additional work required on your part. You can tell the commands that lead to a dialog box because they are followed by ellipses (...) in the drop-down menu.

You can issue commands in Excel yet another way. Right-clicking (clicking the right mouse button) an object, an individual cell, or a selected range of cells displays a shortcut menu that lists common commands that are appropriate to the selection. The following figure shows the shortcut menu that appears when you right-click after selecting a range of cells.

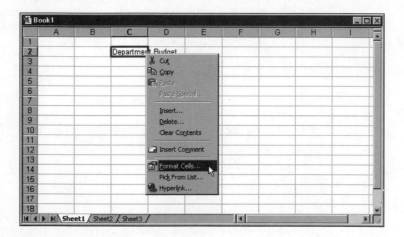

Working with Dialog Boxes

Excel, like virtually every other Windows application, is big on dialog boxes. A *dialog box* is a small window that pops up in response to most of the commands that you issue. This window displays right on top of what you're doing — a sure sign that you must make some type of response to the dialog box before you can do anything else.

The following figure shows a typical Excel dialog box. This particular dialog box displays when you select the File⇨Page Setup command. I chose this for an example because it contains many (but not all) of the types of dialog box controls that you're likely to encounter.

Dialog box parts

Here's a fairly exhaustive list of the various types of controls and other parts you'll meet up with as you discover the world of dialog boxes.

✦ **Button:** Clicking a dialog box button does something else (the "something" depends on the button). If the text on the button has three dots (ellipsis points) after it, clicking the text brings up another dialog box.

✦ **Cancel button:** Click this if you change your mind. None of the changes you made to the dialog box will take effect.

✦ **Check box (not shown):** A square box that you can click to turn the option on or off.

✦ **Drop-down list:** A list of things you can choose from. These lists have a small downward-pointing arrow. Click the arrow to drop the list down and reveal more options.

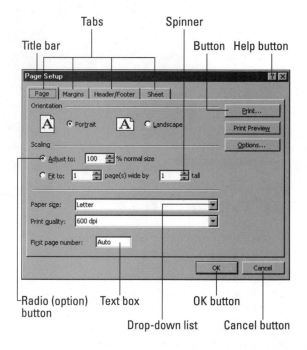

✦ **Help button:** Click here and then click a dialog box control to find out what the control does. Excel displays a pop-up box that describes the control.

✦ **List box (not shown):** This shows several items to choose from and usually has a vertical scroll bar that you can click to show more items in the list.

✦ **OK button:** Click this when you've made your dialog box selections and want to get on with it.

✦ **Radio (option) buttons:** Round buttons, usually enclosed in a group box. Only one option button can be "on" at a time. When you click a radio button, the others in the group turn off.

✦ **Range selector (not shown):** A box that holds a cell or range address. You can click the button to select a range by pointing to it (the dialog box shrinks to get out of your way).

✦ **Spinner:** A control with two arrows (one pointing up, the other pointing down), used in conjunction with a text box. Clicking the arrow increases or decreases the number in the text box.

✦ **Tab:** Clicking a tab changes the dialog box to display a whole new set of controls. Not all dialog boxes have these tabs.

✦ **Text box:** A box in which you enter something — a number or text.

✦ **Text:** Words that explain what to do. You can click dialog box text, but nothing happens.

✦ **Title bar:** The colored bar at the top of the dialog box. Click and drag this to move the dialog box to a different part of the screen if it's covering up something that you want to see.

Navigating through dialog boxes

You can work with a dialog box using your mouse or the keyboard. If you use a mouse, simply position the mouse pointer on the option you want to work with and click. The exact procedure varies with the type of control, but it's quite straightforward — and all Windows programs work the same way.

You'll notice that the various parts of a dialog box have text with a single underlined letter. You can use the Alt key along with this letter to jump to that particular component. For example, the Page Setup dialog box has a text box that's preceded by text that reads, First page number. Because the *r* is underlined, pressing Alt+R puts the cursor in the text box so you can type your option. Besides using Alt key combinations, you can use Tab and Shift+Tab to cycle through all of the controls in a dialog box.

Mousing Around with Toolbars

One of the greatest time-saving features in Excel is its *toolbars*. Excel 2000 comes with 24 toolbars, each of which has a bunch of buttons that provide shortcuts for commonly used commands and procedures. For example, there's a button to left-align the contents of a cell or range. Clicking a button is much faster than issuing the Format⇨Cells command, choosing the Alignment tab, and then selecting the desired option in the dialog box. To make a long story short, it's well worth your effort to learn about the toolbars in Excel.

Understanding the Excel menu bar

In Excel 2000, the menu bar is actually a toolbar. As such, you can move it around on your screen by dragging it. The only difference between the menu bar and any other toolbar is that the menu bar contains drop-down menu items instead of pretty icons.

For each top-level menu item on the Excel 2000 menu bar, there is a "short" and a "long" menu. Excel displays the short menus by default. The short menus show only the most commonly used commands. A small arrow at the foot of the short menu pops open the long version of the menu, with the previously hidden commands shown on a lighter background (holding down a top-level menu item for a few seconds also displays the long menu). When you click one of the normally hidden commands, it is "promoted" and appears thereafter among the commands in the short menu.

If you find the short and long menus confusing, you can turn the "short" and "long" menu option off by choosing View⇨ Toolbars⇨ Customize. Select the Options tab in the Customize dialog box and clear the Menus show recently used commands first check box. (This setting applies to all Office 2000 applications, so if you set it in Excel you automatically set it in Word, PowerPoint, and so on.)

Part II

Using Workbook Files and Worksheets

Working with files is critical to using any software. Microsoft Excel 2000 files are known as *workbooks*. This part covers the procedures that you need to know in order to manage workbook files and use workbooks and worksheets efficiently.

In this part . . .

✔ **Creating, opening, and saving Excel workbooks**

✔ **Importing and exporting files**

✔ **Using workspace and template files**

✔ **Working with sheets in a workbook**

✔ **Exploring workbook navigation techniques**

✔ **Controlling views in windows**

Closing a Workbook

When you're finished using a workbook, use any of these methods to close it and free up the memory it uses.

✦ Use the File➪Close command.

 ✦ Click the Close button in the workbook's title bar (or on the menu bar if the workbook is maximized).

✦ Double-click the Control button in the workbook's title bar (or on the menu bar if the workbook is maximized).

✦ Press Ctrl+F4.

✦ Press Ctrl+W.

If you've made any changes to your workbook since the last time you saved it, Excel asks if you want to save the changes before closing it.

> **TIP**
>
> To close all open workbooks, press the Shift key and choose the File➪Close All command (this command only appears when you hold down the Shift key while you click the File menu). Excel closes each workbook, prompting you for each unsaved workbook.

Creating an Empty Workbook File

When you start Excel, it automatically creates a new (empty) workbook called Book1. If you're starting a new project from scratch you can use this blank workbook.

You can create another blank workbook in any of three ways:

✦ Click the New button on the Standard toolbar.

✦ Press Ctrl+N.

✦ Select File➪New and double-click the Workbook icon in the General tab of the New dialog box.

Any of these methods creates a blank default workbook.

Creating a Workbook from a Template

A *template* is a workbook that's all set up with formulas and ready for you to enter data. The Spreadsheet Solutions templates distributed with Excel are nicely formatted and relatively easy to customize.

To create a workbook from a template, follow these steps:

1. Select the File⇨New command.

Excel responds by displaying the New dialog box.

2. Select the template that you want.

The New dialog box has several tabs. Clicking a tab displays additional templates.

3. Click OK to open a copy of the template.

Creating a Workbook Template

A *workbook template* is a normal workbook that is used as the basis for other workbooks. A workbook template can use any of Excel's features such as charts, formulas, and macros. Normally, you set up a template so that you can enter some values and get immediate results. Excel includes several templates, and you can create your own.

To save a workbook as a template, follow these steps:

1. Choose the File⇨Save As command.

2. Select Template from the drop-down list box labeled Save as type.

Excel displays the Templates folder in the Save-in drop-down list box.

3. Save the template in your Templates folder (or a subfolder within the Templates folder).

Deleting a Workbook File

When you no longer need a workbook file, you may want to delete it from your disk to free up space and reduce the number of files displayed in the Open dialog box.

You can delete files using standard Windows techniques, or you can delete files directly from Excel.

1. Use either the File⇨Open command or the File⇨Save As command to bring up a dialog box with a list of filenames.

2. Right-click a filename and choose Delete from the shortcut menu. Depending on how your system is set up, you may have to confirm this action.

If your system is set up to use the Recycle Bin, you may be able to recover a file that you delete accidentally. Before you empty the Recycle Bin, open it up and drag out any items you wish to save.

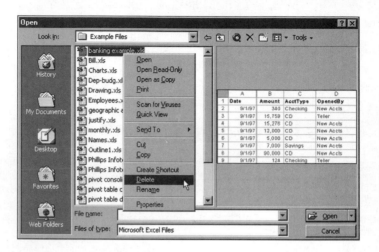

Exporting a Text File

If you want to save information in a worksheet so that it can be used by other programs that can't read Excel files directly, you can export your worksheet as a text file. Most applications can read text files. To export a worksheet as a text file, follow these steps:

1. Choose the File⇨Save As command.

2. Select one of the following file types from the Save as type drop-down list box: Formatted text, Text, or CSV.

   CSV stands for *comma-separated value.*

3. Click Save to create the text file.

When you save a workbook as a text file, be aware that text files simply contain data. These files have no formulas, formatting, or charts.

If you want to save your formulas to a text file, you can. Select Tools⇨ Options and click to place a check mark in the Formulas check box. This action displays formulas (instead of their resultant values) in your spread sheet. Then save your spreadsheet as a text file.

In some cases you may be able to use the Office Clipboard to copy data from Excel and paste it directly to the other application.

Importing a Text File

To import a text file into Excel, follow these steps:

1. Choose the Data⇨Get External Data⇨Import Text File command. This command displays the Import Text File dialog box.

2. The drop-down list box labeled Files of type displays text files that have a TXT extension. If the text file that you're importing doesn't have a TXT extension, select the All Files option.

3. Select the file and click Import.

4. Click Finish when you have completed the steps in the Text Import Wizard. The Import Data dialog box now appears.

5. In the Import Data dialog box, select where you want to put the data and click OK to complete the import.

Excel examines the file.

✦ If the file is a tab-delimited or a comma-separated value (CSV) file, Excel often imports it with no further intervention on your part.

If you import text files from countries other than the U.S., you can change the decimal and/or thousands separator for numeric values to be imported if required. To change the decimal and/or thousands separator, click the Advanced button in Step 3 of 3 of the Text Import Wizard and make your changes in the Advanced Text Import Settings dialog box that pops up.

✦ If the file can be imported in several different ways or if there are no delimiters, Excel displays its Text Import Wizard (a series of interactive dialog boxes in which you specify the information needed to break the lines of the text file into the columns). Follow the steps outlined in the Text Import Wizard dialog box to help separate the file into columns. The Text Import Wizard contains a preview box that shows you how the data will be imported.

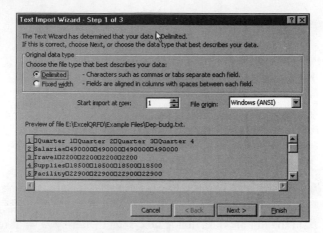

If you import a lot of text files in the same format, you can avoid repeating the import procedure for each file by creating a "refreshable" text import template. Follow these steps to create the template:

1. When the Import Data dialog box is displayed (see Step 5 of Importing a Text File), click Properties. This displays the External Data Range Properties dialog box.

2. Select the options you want in the External Data Range Properties dialog box. To preserve the import settings you defined in the Text Import Wizard, make sure that the Save query definition box is checked. Click OK when you complete your selections.

3. To see a description of the options in the External Data Range Properties dialog box, right click an option and click the What's This? box that pops up.

Click OK when you complete your selections.

4. Click OK in the Import Data dialog box to import the file.

5. Select the File⇨Save As command and enter a filename in the File name list box. In the list box labeled Save as type, choose Template. Click Save to save the template.

- If you do not check any Refresh options in the External Data Range Properties dialog box, when you open the template you can refresh your data by selecting the Data⇨Refresh Data command.

- If you wish to update data in the same file, in Step 5 save the file as an Excel Workbook instead of a Template.

See also "Creating a Workbook Template," in this part.

Opening a Non-Excel File

To open a non-Excel file, follow these steps:

1. Choose File⇨Open to bring up the Open dialog box.

2. Select the file type from the Files of type drop-down list box.

3. Specify the folder that contains the file.

4. Select the file and click Open or double-click the filename.

File Type	Description
WKS	1-2-3 Release 1 spreadsheet format*
WKS	MS Works 2.0 format*
WK1	1-2-3 Release 2 spreadsheet format**
WK3	1-2-3 Release 3 spreadsheet format**
WK4	1-2-3 for Windows spreadsheet format
WQ1	Quattro Pro for DOS spreadsheet format
WB1	Quattro Pro 1.0/5.0 for Windows spreadsheet format*
DBF	dBase database format
SLK	SYLK spreadsheet format
CSV	Comma-separated value text file format
TXT	Text file format
PRN	Text file format
DIF	Data Interchange Format
HTM	HTML documents
IQR	Web query format*
DQY	Database query format (MS Query 97 and higher)*
OQY	OLAP query format*
QRY	Database query format (pre-MS Query 97)

Excel can open files in this format but not save them.

**When you open one of these files, Excel searches for the associated formatting file (either FMT or FM3) and attempts to translate the formatting.*

Opening a Workbook File

Excel's primary file type is called a *workbook file*. When you open a workbook in Excel, the entire file is loaded into memory, and any changes that you make occur only in the copy that's in memory.

To open an existing workbook file, follow these steps:

1. Choose File⇨Open to bring up the Open dialog box.

You can also use any of the following methods to bring up the Open dialog box:

- Click the Open button on the Standard toolbar.
- Press Ctrl+O.
- Press Ctrl+F12 (or Ctrl+Alt+F2 if your keyboard lacks an F12 function key).

2. Specify the folder that contains the file.

3. Select the workbook file and click Open or double-click the filename.

You can select more than one file in the Open dialog box. The trick is to hold down the Ctrl key while you click the filenames. After you select all of the files you want, click Open.

Excel 2000 comes with a new "Web browser-style" Open dialog box. On the left-hand side of the dialog box is a vertical toolbar for quick access to commonly used folders. The blue arrow in the toolbar functions like a browser's back button. In the dialog box's toolbar, clicking the arrow takes you back to folders viewed previously.

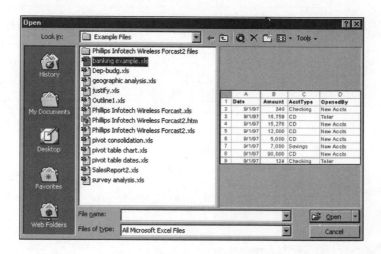

The following are other ways to open a workbook file:

✦ Double-click the workbook icon in any folder window. If Excel is not running, it starts automatically. Or you can drag a workbook icon into the Excel window to load the workbook.

✦ Excel provides a list of files you've worked with recently at the bottom of the File menu. If the file you want appears in this list, you can choose it directly from the menu.

✦ If the workbook contains macros, you may be asked if you want to disable the macros. This is a simple form of virus protection. (Disable the macros if you are unsure of the origin of the workbook or are suspicious that it may contain a virus.)

✦ If you find that you use the same workbook every time you start Excel, you can make this workbook open automatically whenever Excel starts. Just move the workbook to the Excel\Xlstart folder or to the Program Files\Microsoft Office\Office\XLStart folder — or to wherever your Xlstart folder may be.

Protecting a Workbook File

Sometimes, you may want to protect a workbook by preventing users from adding or deleting sheets. Or, you may want to ensure that the workbook's window size or position is not changed.

1. Choose the Tools⇨Protection⇨Protect Workbook command to display the following dialog box.

2. Choose the appropriate option and click OK.

• Structure prevents any of the following changes to a workbook: Adding a sheet, deleting a sheet, moving a sheet, renaming a sheet, hiding a sheet, or unhiding a sheet.

• Windows protects the workbook window from being moved or resized.

3. You can supply a password or not, depending on the level of protection you need.

To remove protection from a protected workbook, choose the Tools⇨Protection⇨Unprotect Workbook command.

Protecting a Worksheet

Deleting a single formula on a worksheet often has a ripple effect, causing other formulas to produce an error value or, even worse, incorrect results. You can circumvent such problems by locking the cells you don't want to be modified and then protecting your worksheets from being modified:

1. Choose the Tools⇨Protection⇨Protect Sheet command.

   The Protect Sheet dialog box appears.

2. Choose the appropriate option or options and click OK.

   • **Contents:** Selecting this option prevents the cell from being changed.

   • **Objects:** Selecting this option prevents drawing objects (including embedded charts) from being changed.

   • **Scenarios:** Selecting this option prevents defined scenarios from being changed (*see* "Performing What-If Analysis," in Part VI).

3. Provide a password in the Protect Sheet dialog box, if you'd like:

   • If you enter a password, the password must be reentered before the sheet can be unprotected.

   • If you don't supply a password, anyone can unprotect the sheet.

Remember: By default, all cells are locked. Before protecting a worksheet, you normally want to unlock the input cells. You can lock or unlock a cell or object by accessing its Format dialog box and clicking the Protection tab. (For more information, see *Excel 2000 For Windows For Dummies* by Greg Harvey, from IDG Books Worldwide, Inc.)

You can't change a cell's locked status while the worksheet is protected. You must unprotect the sheet to make any changes and then protect it again. To remove protection from a protected sheet, choose the Tools⇨Protection⇨Unprotect Sheet command.

Saving a Workbook File

When you save a workbook, Excel saves the copy in memory to your disk — overwriting the previous copy of the file. When you save a workbook for the first time, Excel displays its Save As dialog box.

To save the active workbook to disk, follow these steps:

1. Choose the File➪Save command.

You may prefer to use any of the following methods to save:

- Click the Save button on the Standard toolbar
- Press the Ctrl+S shortcut key combination
- Press the Shift+F12 shortcut key combination

If the file has not yet been saved, Excel prompts you for a name using its Save As dialog box.

2. Select the folder that will hold the file.

3. Enter a name in the File name box. (A filename can consist of as many as 255 characters, including spaces.)

4. Click Save.

You should save your work at a time interval that corresponds to the maximum amount of time that you're willing to lose. For example, if you don't mind losing an hour's work, save your file every hour. Most people save at more frequent intervals. *See also* "Saving your work automatically," in this part.

Saving a workbook under a different name

Sometimes, you may want to keep multiple versions of your work by saving each successive version under a different name.

To save a workbook with a different name, follow these steps:

1. Use File➪Save As to display the Save As dialog box.

2. Select the folder in which to store the workbook.

3. Enter a new filename in the File name box.

4. Click Save.

A new copy is created with a different name, but the original version of the file remains intact.

You can also use the File➪Save As command to make a backup copy of a workbook simply by saving the file (with the same name) to a floppy disk, a different drive, or a different folder. Excel remembers the last place that it was saved, so you may want to save the workbook again in its original location.

If you would like to prevent others from opening a workbook or from making changes to it, select the Tools➪General Options command in the Save As dialog box and enter a password in the Save Options dialog box.

Saving a workbook file in an older Excel format

If you need to share a file with someone who uses an older version of Excel, make sure you save the file in a format that the earlier version of Excel can read.

To save a workbook for an earlier version of Excel, follow these steps:

1. Choose the File⇨Save As command.

2. In the drop-down list box labeled Save as type, choose the format to save the file in.

3. Click Save.

Excel 5 and Excel 95 use the same file format; Excel 2000 and Excel 97 use the same file format.

Remember: Excel 5 was the first version to use multisheet workbooks. Prior to Excel 5, worksheets, chart sheets, and macro sheets were all stored in separate files. Consequently, if you share a multisheet workbook with someone who still uses one of these older versions, you must save each sheet separately — and in the proper format.

Remember: Be careful if you plan to share a worksheet file with someone who doesn't use Windows 95 or Windows NT. Older versions of Windows don't support long filenames, so the filename may appear truncated.

Saving a workbook as a Web page

Excel 2000 uses HTML as a native file format. When you save your file in this format, all of your original text formatting, cell formatting, added charts, embedded images, and so on remain intact when you reopen the file in Excel.

Saving the file in HTML format allows the file to be viewed in a Web browser.

To save your file as a Web page, follow these steps:

1. Select the File⇨Save As Web Page command.

2. In the Save As dialog box, select Entire Workbook (Entire Workbook is the default setting).

3. Select the folder or Web server where you wish to store the workbook.

4. If you wish to change the saved filename, enter a new filename in the File name box.

5. Click Save.

The file is saved with an HTM extension.

Remember: You may not be able to view all of the formatting options applied to your document when the file is opened in a Web browser because Excel embeds additional information into the document that describes complex formatting options in the HTML file. Many browsers are unable to interpret this additional information.

Remember: Excel applies certain defaults when saving your HTML file. You can change these defaults by selecting Tools⇨Options, clicking the General tab, and clicking the Web Options button.

You can preview the file before you save it by selecting the File⇨Web Page Preview command. *See also* "Web Publishing," in Part VII, for more information on saving a workbook as a Web page and for a description of the options in the Web Options dialog box.

Saving your work automatically

If you're the type who gets so wrapped up in your work that you forget to save your file on a regular basis, you may be interested in Excel's AutoSave feature. AutoSave automatically saves your workbook at a pre-specified interval.

Using the AutoSave feature requires that you load an add-in file that is included with Excel, but not normally installed. To install the AutoSave Add-in, do the following:

1. Select Tools⇨add-Ins to display the Add-Ins dialog box.

2. Click AutoSave Add-in in the list of add-ins and then click OK.

The add-in will be installed every time you run Excel. If you want to permanently remove the AutoSave feature, repeat the process and uncheck the Autosave Add-in check box. If you want to temporarily disable the AutoSave feature, select Tools⇨AutoSave. In the AutoSave dialog box, clear the Automatic Save Every check box.

You only have to install the Add-in once. If you tire of the AutoSave feature you can turn it off without having to uninstall it. Select Tools⇨AutoSave. In the AutoSave dialog box that appears, clear the check mark from the Automatic Save Every check box. Repeat this procedure to turn AutoSave on again.

Remember: After the AutoSave feature is installed, the Tools menu contains a new menu item: AutoSave. Selecting the Tools⇨ AutoSave command displays the AutoSave dialog box in which you specify your options.

Using a Default Worksheet Template

A default sheet template is used as the basis for a new worksheet you add to a workbook. You can create a custom default sheet template by following these steps:

1. Create a new workbook that contains one worksheet. If your new workbooks contain three worksheets (the Excel default amount), select Sheet2; then hold down the Shift (or Ctrl) key and select Sheet3. Right click one of the selected sheets and choose delete from the shortcut menu.

If you have more than three worksheets in your new workbooks, select Sheet2; then hold down the Shift key and select the last worksheet. This procedure selects all sheets between Sheet2 and the last sheet inclusive. As before, choosing delete from the shortcut menu deletes all the selected sheets.

2. Apply the desired formatting, text, and styles to the worksheet.

3. Select Program Files\Microsoft Office\Office\XLStart.

4. Select File⇨Save As and click Template in the Save as type box.

5. In the File name box, type **sheet.xlt**.

6. Click Save.

All new worksheets that you add to any workbook will now be a replica of the sheet you created in Step 2.

You can always edit the sheet.xlt file, or delete it if you no longer want to use it.

See also "Using a Default Workbook Template," in this part.

Using a Default Workbook Template

A default workbook template is used as the basis for all new workbooks you create. You can create a custom default workbook template by following these steps:

1. Create a new workbook.

2. Add or delete as many worksheets as you want to appear in new workbooks.

3. Apply the desired formatting, sheet names, text, style, and so on.

4. Select the Program Files\Microsoft Office\Office\XLStart folder.

5. Select File⇨Save As and click Template in the Save as type box.

6. In the File name box, type **book.xlt**.

7. Click Save.

All new workbooks that you create will now be a replica of the workbook you created in Step 3.

You can always edit the book.xlt file, or delete it if you no longer want to use it.

See also "Using a Default Worksheet Template," in this part.

Using a Workspace File

Workspace means all of the workbooks and their screen positions and window sizes — sort of a snapshot of Excel's current state.

You may have a project that uses two or more workbooks, and you may also like to arrange the windows in a certain way to make it easy to access them. Fortunately, Excel lets you save your entire workspace to a file. Then you can open the workspace file, and Excel is set up exactly as it was when you saved your workspace.

Saving a workspace file

1. Choose the File⇨Save Workspace command.

2. You can use the proposed name (resume.xlw or resume) or enter a different name in the File name field.

The file extension shows up only if you turn off the Hide file extensions for known file types option in the on the View tab of the Folder Options dialog box in Windows Explorer. This option is turned on by default.

3. Click the Save button and the workspace is saved to a disk.

A workspace file does not include the workbook files themselves — only the information needed to recreate the workspace. The workbooks are saved in standard workbook files. Therefore, if you distribute a workspace file to a coworker, make sure that you also include the workbook files that the workspace file refers to.

If you save your workspace file in the XLStart folder, Excel opens the workspace file automatically when it starts up. But a word of caution may be in order here. Excel will attempt to open any and all files located in the XLStart folder when it starts up.

Opening a workspace file

To open a workspace file, choose the File⇨Open command and select the workspace file in the Open dialog box. Excel opens all of the workbooks that you originally saved in the workspace.

Working with Worksheets

A workbook can consist of any number of *worksheets*. Each sheet has a tab that appears at the bottom of the workbook window. To activate a different sheet, just click its tab. If the tab for the sheet that you want to activate is not visible, use the tab scrolling buttons to scroll the sheet tabs.

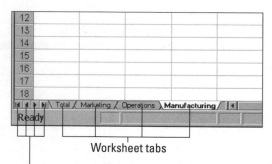

Worksheet tabs

Tab scrolling buttons

Remember: If a sheet is hidden, its tab is also hidden. Before you can activate a hidden sheet, use the Format⇨Sheet⇨Unhide command to unhide it.

You also can use these shortcut keys to activate a different sheet:

✦ **Ctrl+PgUp:** Activates the previous sheet, if there is one.

✦ **Ctrl+PgDn:** Activates the next sheet, if there is one.

Adding a new worksheet

You can add a new worksheet to a workbook in three ways:

✦ Select the Insert⇨Worksheet command.

+ Right-click a sheet tab, choose Insert from the shortcut menu, and select Worksheet from the General tab in the Insert dialog box.

+ Press Shift+F11.

Excel inserts a new worksheet before the active worksheet; the new worksheet then becomes the active worksheet.

Arranging windows automatically

If you want all of your unhidden workbook windows to be visible, you can move and resize them manually — or you can let Excel do it automatically.

Window⇨Arrange displays a dialog box that lists the four window arrangement options. Just select the one that you want and click OK.

Changing a sheet's name

Worksheets, by default, are named Sheet1, Sheet2, and so on. Providing more meaningful names helps you identify a particular sheet. To change a sheet's name, use any of these methods:

+ Choose the Format⇨Sheet⇨Rename command.

+ Double-click the sheet tab.

+ Right-click the sheet tab and choose the Rename command from the shortcut menu.

Any of these methods selects the text in the tab. Just type the new sheet name directly on the tab.

Sheet names can be up to 31 characters. Spaces are allowed, but the following characters are not: [] (square brackets); : (colon); / (slash);\ (backslash); ? (question mark); and * (asterisk).

Keep in mind that the name you give is displayed on the sheet tab; a longer name results in a wider tab. Therefore, if you use lengthy sheet names, you can see fewer sheet tabs without scrolling.

Changing a window's size (maximizing, minimizing, and restoring)

A workbook window in Excel can be in any of three states:

+ Maximized to fill Excel's entire workspace. A maximized window does not have a title bar, and the workbook's name appears in the Excel title bar. To maximize a window, click its Maximize button. Or you can double-click its title bar.

✦ Minimized to appear as a small window with only a title bar. To minimize a window, click its Minimize button.

 ✦ Restored to a non-maximized size. To restore a window, click its Restore button.

You can also use the following key combinations:

Key Combination	Action
Ctrl+F5	Restores a window
Ctrl+F9	Minimizes a window
Ctrl+F10	Maximizes a window

When you maximize one window, all the other windows are maximized, too (but you can't see them).

 Many users prefer to do most of their work with maximized workbook windows. This lets you see more cells and eliminates the distraction of other workbook windows getting in the way.

Copying a worksheet

You can make an exact copy of a worksheet — and put it either in its original workbook or in a different workbook — in one of two ways:

✦ Select the Edit⇨Move or Copy Sheet command. Select the location for the copy and make sure that the check box labeled Create a Copy is checked. Click OK to make the copy.

✦ Click the sheet tab, press Ctrl, and drag it to its desired location. When you drag, the mouse pointer changes to a small sheet with a plus sign on it.

If necessary, Excel changes the name of the copied sheet to make it unique within the workbook. For example, if you copy a sheet named Sheet1 to a workbook that already has a sheet named Sheet1, Excel changes the name to Sheet1 (2). To change the name of a sheet *see* "Changing a sheet's name," earlier in this part.

Creating multiple windows (views) for a workbook

Sometimes, you may like to view two different parts of a worksheet at once. Or you may want to see more than one sheet in the same workbook. You can accomplish either of these actions by displaying your workbook in one or more additional windows.

To create a new view of the active workbook choose Window⇨New Window. Excel displays a new window for the active workbook. To help you keep track of the windows, Excel appends a colon and a number to each window.

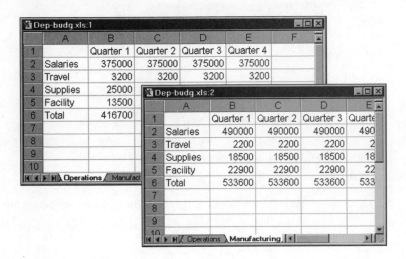

Remember: A single workbook can have as many views (that is, separate windows) as you like.

Displaying multiple windows for a workbook also makes it easier to copy information from one worksheet to another. You can use Excel's drag-and-drop procedures to copy a cell, a range, a graphic object, or a chart.

Creating and using named views

Excel lets you name various *views* of your worksheet and to switch quickly among these named views. A view includes settings for window size and position, frozen panes or titles, outlining, zoom factor, the active cell, print area, and many of the settings in the Options dialog box. A view can also include hidden print settings and hidden rows and columns.

To create a named view, follow these steps:

1. Set up the worksheet the way you want it to appear.

2. Select the View⇨Custom Views command.

3. In the Custom Views dialog box, click the Add button and then enter a descriptive name for the view.

To display a view that you've named, select the View⇨Custom Views command, select the view from the list, and click the Show button.

Deleting a worksheet

You can delete a worksheet in one of two ways:

✦ Activate the sheet and select the Edit⇨Delete Sheet command.

✦ Right-click the sheet tab and choose the Delete command from the shortcut menu.

In either case, Excel asks you to confirm the fact that you want to delete the sheet. Every workbook must have at least one sheet so, if you try to delete the only sheet, Excel will complain.

To select multiple sheets to delete, press Ctrl while clicking the sheet tabs that you want to delete. To select a group of contiguous sheets, click the first sheet tab, press Shift, and then click the last sheet tab.

When you delete a worksheet, it's gone for good. This is one of the few operations in Excel that can't be undone. You may want to save a workbook before deleting worksheets. Then, if you inadvertently delete a worksheet, you can revert to the saved version.

Freezing row or column titles

Many worksheets (such as budgets) are set up with row and column headings. When you scroll through such a worksheet, it's very easy to get lost when the row and column headings scroll out of view. Excel provides a handy solution: freezing rows and/or columns.

To freeze rows or columns, follow these steps:

1. Move the cell pointer to the cell below the row that you want to freeze and to the right of the column that you want to freeze. For example, to freeze row 1 and column A, move the cell pointer to cell B2.

2. Select the Window➪Freeze Panes command.

Excel inserts dark lines to indicate the frozen rows and columns. These frozen rows and columns remain visible as you scroll throughout the worksheet.

To remove the frozen rows or columns, select the Window➪ Unfreeze Panes command. *See also* "Splitting panes," in this part.

Hiding and unhiding a worksheet

Hiding a worksheet is useful if you don't want others to see it or if you just want to get it out of the way. When a sheet is hidden, its sheet tab is hidden also.

To hide a worksheet, choose the Format➪Sheet➪Hide command. The active worksheet (or selected worksheets) is hidden from view.

Remember: Every workbook must have at least one visible sheet, so Excel doesn't allow you to hide all sheets in a workbook.

To unhide a hidden worksheet, follow these steps:

1. Choose the Format➪Sheet➪Unhide command. A dialog box pops up listing all hidden sheets.

2. Choose the sheet that you want to unhide and click OK.

See also "Adding a new worksheet," in this part.

Moving a sheet

Sometimes, you want to rearrange the order of worksheets in a workbook — or move a sheet to a different workbook.

First, select the sheet that you want to move by clicking the sheet tab. You can also move multiple sheets at once by selecting them: Press Ctrl while you click the sheet tabs that you want to move.

There are two ways to move a selected worksheet(s):

✦ Select the Edit➪Move or Copy Sheet command. The Move or Copy dialog box pops up asking you to select the workbook and the new location.

✦ Click the sheet tab and drag it to its desired location (either in the same workbook or in a different workbook). When you drag, the mouse pointer changes to a small sheet, and a small arrow guides you. To move a worksheet to a different workbook, both workbooks must be open.

Remember: If you move a worksheet to a workbook that already has a sheet with the same name, Excel changes the name to make it unique. For example, if you move a sheet named Sheet1 to a workbook that already has a sheet named Sheet1, Excel changes the name to Sheet1 (2). To change the name of a sheet *see* "Changing a sheet's name," earlier in this part.

Moving and resizing windows

To move a window, first make sure that it is not maximized. If it is maximized, click its Restore button (shown in the margin). Move the window by clicking and dragging its title bar with your mouse. Note that the window can extend off-screen in any direction, if you like.

To resize a window, click and drag any of its borders until it's the size you want it to be. When you position the mouse pointer on a window's border, the mouse pointer changes shape (to a double arrow) to let you know that you can then click and drag. To resize a window horizontally and vertically at the same time, click and drag any of its corners.

Moving around in a worksheet

Navigating through a worksheet with a mouse works just as you would expect. Just click a cell and it becomes the active cell. If the cell that you want to activate is not visible in the workbook window, you can use the scroll bars to scroll the window in any direction.

✦ To scroll one cell, click one of the arrows on the scroll bar.

✦ To scroll by a complete screen, click either side of the scroll bar's slider button (the large center button).

✦ To scroll faster, drag the slider.

✦ To scroll a long distance vertically, hold down the Shift key while dragging the slider button.

Notice that only the active workbook window has scroll bars. When you activate a different window, the scroll bars appear.

When you drag the scroll bar's slider, a small box appears that tells you which row or column you will scroll to when you release your finger from the mouse.

Remember: Using the scroll bars doesn't change the active cell. It simply scrolls the worksheet. To change the active cell, you must click on a new cell after scrolling.

Your mouse may be equipped with a small wheel (Microsoft's IntelliMouse is an example). If you have such a mouse, you can spin the wheel to scroll vertically. If this doesn't work, select Tools⇨Options, click the General tab, and remove the check mark from Zoom on roll with IntelliMouse.

Splitting panes

Splitting a window into two or four panes lets you view multiple parts of the same worksheet.

✦ The Window⇨Split command splits the active worksheet into two or four separate panes.

✦ The split occurs at the location of the cell pointer.

✦ You can use the mouse to drag the pane and resize it.

✦ To remove the split panes, choose Window⇨Remove Split.

A faster way to split and unsplit panes is to drag either the vertical or horizontal split bar, shown in the following figure. To remove split panes using the mouse, drag the pane separator all the way to the edge of the window or just double-click it.

Vertical split bar   Horizontal split bar

	A	B	C		J	K	L	M	
1									
2									
3									
4									
5									
6									
17									
18									
19									
20									
21									

Book3 — Sheet1 / Sheet2

See also "Freezing row or column titles," in this part.

Using full screen view

If you would like to see as much information as possible, Excel offers a full screen view. Choose the View⇨Full Screen command, and Excel maximizes its window and removes all elements except the menu bar. Choose View⇨Full Screen again to return to normal.

Zooming worksheets

If you have a Microsoft IntelliMouse, or equivalent device, you can zoom out on a worksheet by pressing Ctrl while you move the mouse wheel. Make sure the Zoom on roll with IntelliMouse option is selected in the Options dialog box (select the Tools⇨Options command and click the General tab).

The easiest way to change the zoom factor of the active worksheet is to use the Zoom control on the Standard toolbar. Just click on the arrow and select the desired zoom factor from the list. Your screen transforms immediately. (You can also choose View⇨Zoom to bring up the Zoom dialog box, or type a number directly into the Zoom box on the Standard toolbar.)

Zoom control

The Selection option in the toolbar Zoom control drop-down list zooms the worksheet to display only the selected cells. This option is useful if you want to view only a particular range. For finer control over the zoom factor you can click the Zoom control, enter a zoom factor directly, and press Enter.

Part III

Formatting, Outlining, and Printing Your Work

The end result of most spreadsheet work is the printed page that you can take to your boss for detailed data analysis. This part deals with topics related to formatting your work to get it ready for printing, creating outlines, and printing your worksheet in Microsoft Excel 2000.

In this part . . .

- ✓ Using different type fonts, sizes, and attributes
- ✓ Adding borders around cells
- ✓ Changing the way cell contents are aligned within cells
- ✓ Changing colors (and patterns) in your worksheet
- ✓ Adjusting row heights and column widths
- ✓ Changing the way numbers look
- ✓ Creating and using worksheet outlines
- ✓ Setting options for printing
- ✓ Previewing your work before you print it
- ✓ Printing worksheets

Formatting Cells and Ranges

You have lots of control over the appearance of information that you enter into a cell. Changing the appearance of cell contents is known as *formatting*. Excel provides four ways to format cells:

+ **Toolbar buttons:** Common formatting commands are available on toolbar buttons on the Formatting toolbar.

+ **Shortcut keys:** Some common formats can be applied by pressing shortcut key combinations. For example, Ctrl+B makes the text bold.

+ **The Format Cells dialog box:** This tabbed dialog box provides all of the cell formatting commands. Click one of the six tabs to access a particular panel in the dialog box.

+ **The AutoFormat dialog box:** Provides 16 "canned" formats from which to choose. Select Format⇨AutoFormat to display this dialog box.

You can bring up the Format Cells dialog box in any of three ways:

+ Choose the Format⇨Cells command.

+ Press Ctrl+1 when a cell or range is selected.

+ Right-click the selected cell or range of cells and choose Format Cells from the shortcut menu.

You can format cells before or after you enter information. For example, if you're entering a series of numbers, you can preformat the cells so the numbers will appear with commas and the desired number of decimal places.

Remember: Formatting does not affect the contents of your worksheet — only the way the text and values appear in the cell and in any succeeding printouts.

Adding borders to a cell or range

Borders often are used to "group" a range of similar cells or simply as a way to delineate rows or columns for aesthetic purposes.

To add borders around a cell or range, follow these steps:

1. Select the cell or range.

2. Choose the Format⇨Cells command (or press Ctrl+1).

3. Click the Border tab in the Format Cells dialog box.

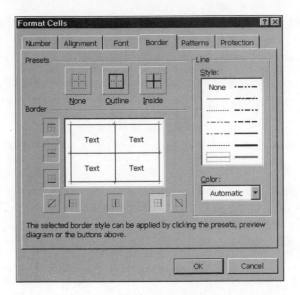

4. Select a line style from the <u>S</u>tyle portion of the dialog box.

5. Select the border position for the line style by clicking one of the buttons.

These buttons are *toggles* (they either add or remove the border). Excel displays the selected border style in the dialog box. You can choose different styles for different border positions. You can also select a color for the border.

6. Click OK to apply the borders to your selection.

The three buttons labeled Presets let you quickly remove all borders, add a border around the outside of the selection, or add borders to the interior of the selection. You can also apply diagonal borders that extend through cells and ranges. Diagonal borders give the effect of the cells being "crossed out."

If you use border formatting in your worksheet, you may want to turn off the grid display to make the borders more pronounced. Select <u>T</u>ools⇨<u>O</u>ptions, click the View panel of the Options dialog box, and remove the check mark from the <u>G</u>ridlines option.

Remember: Applying a border to the bottom of a cell is not the same as applying the underline attribute to the font. These two operations result in quite different effects.

See also "Changing text attributes," in this part.

Aligning cell contents

By default, cell contents appear at the bottom, numbers are right-aligned, text is left-aligned, and logical values are centered in cells.

You can apply the most common horizontal alignment options by selecting the cell or range of cells and using the tools on the Formatting toolbar: Align Left, Center, and Align Right. *See also* "Indenting the contents of a cell," in this part.

You can use the following procedure to align cell contents:

1. Select the cell or range of cells to align.

2. Choose the Format⇨Cells command (or press Ctrl+1).

3. Click the Alignment tab in the Format Cells dialog box.

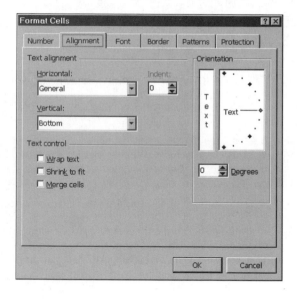

4. Choose the desired horizontal or vertical alignment option from the drop-down lists.

5. Click OK.

Applying background colors and patterns

To change the background color or pattern used in cells, follow these steps:

1. Select the cell or range that you want to format.

2. Choose the Format⇨Cells command (or press Ctrl+1).

3. Click the Patterns tab in the Format Cells dialog box.

4. Choose a color from the Color section.

5. To add a pattern, click the Pattern drop-down box and choose a pattern.

If you like, you can choose a second color for the pattern.

6. Click OK to apply the color and/or pattern.

Remember: If you use background colors or patterns, you may not receive the results you want if you print with a non-color printer.

See also "Printing colors in black and white," in this part.

A faster way to change the background color (but not a pattern) is to select the cells and then select a color from the Fill Color tool on the Formatting toolbar.

Applying a background graphic

In some cases you may want to use a graphics file as a background for a worksheet — similar to the *wallpaper* you may display on your Windows desktop.

To add a background to a worksheet, follow these steps:

1. Activate the worksheet.

2. Choose the Format➪Sheet➪Background command.

Excel displays a dialog box that lets you choose a graphics file.

3. Locate the desired graphics file (you may have to change to a different folder).

4. Click Insert, and Excel tiles your worksheet with the graphic you selected.

In some cases, adding a graphic background makes it difficult to view text in cells, so you may have to use colored text or apply a background color to the non-empty cells. You'll want to turn off the gridline display because the gridlines show through the graphic.

To get rid of a background graphic, use the Format➪Sheet➪Delete Background command.

Remember: The graphic background is for the screen display only; it doesn't show up on the page when you print the worksheet.

Applying colors to text

Following is the fastest way to change the color of text:

1. Select the cell or range.

 2. Select a color from the Font Color tool on the Formatting toolbar.

> If you click the down arrow button on the Font Color tool, it expands to show more colors.

You can also change text color in the Font panel of the Format Cells dialog box.

Applying named styles

Excel lets you associate a named style with any cell. By default, all cells have the Normal style. In addition, Excel provides five other built-in styles — all of which control only the cell's number format. The styles available in every workbook are listed in the following table.

Style Name	Description	Number Format Example
Normal	Excel's default style	1234
Comma*	Comma with two decimal places	1,234.00
Comma[0]	Comma with no decimal places	1,234
Currency*	Left-aligned dollar sign with comma and two decimal places	$ 1,234.00
Currency[0]	Left-aligned dollar sign with comma and no decimal places	$ 1,234
Percent*	Percent with no decimal places	12%

* This style can be applied by clicking a button on the Standard toolbar.

 Excel also lets you create your own styles (for both numbers and text). To apply a custom style or a style that isn't associated with a toolbar button, do the following:

1. Select the cell or range that you want to apply the style to.

2. Choose Format⇨Style.

> Excel displays its Style dialog box.

3. Select the style from the Style Name drop-down box.

> This list will display the Excel built-in styles and your own styles (if any).

4. Click OK to apply the style to the selection.

See also "Creating and modifying named styles," in this part.

Changing column width

You may want to change the width of a column if it's not wide enough to display values fully (you get a series of pound signs: #######), or simply to space out the cells horizontally. Before changing the width, you can select a number of columns so that the selected columns will all have the same width.

Use any of these methods to change the width of selected columns.

   ✦ Choose the Format⇨Column⇨Width command and enter a value in the Column Width dialog box.

   ✦ Drag the right border of the column heading with the mouse until the column is the desired width.

   ✦ Choose the Format⇨Column⇨AutoFit Selection command. This adjusts the width of the selected column(s) so that the widest entry in the column fits.

   ✦ Double-click the right border of a column heading to automatically set the column width to the widest entry in the column.

To change the default width of all columns, use the Format⇨Column⇨Standard Width command. This displays a dialog box into which you enter the new default column width. All columns that haven't been previously adjusted take on the new column width.

Changing the default font (typeface)

If you want to change the typeface used in all of the cells in a workbook, change the definition for the Normal style:

1. Select Format⇨Style.

   Excel displays its Style dialog box.

2. Select Normal from the drop-down list named Style Name.

3. Click the Modify button to display the Format Cells dialog box.

4. Click the Font tab in the Format Cells dialog box.

5. Select the font that you want to be the default.

6. Click OK twice.

Remember: Changing the Normal style affects only the current workbook. To change the font used for all of your workbooks, select Tools⇨Options, click the General tab in the Options dialog box, and modify the Standard font and Size settings.

Changing fonts and text sizes

The easiest way to change the font or text size for selected cells is to use the Font and Font Size tools on the Formatting toolbar. Just select the cells, click the appropriate tool, and select the font or size from the drop-down list.

You can also use the following technique, which lets you control several other properties of the font from a single dialog box:

1. Select the cell or range to modify.

2. Choose the Format➪Cells command (or press Ctrl+1).

3. Click the Font tab in the Format Cells dialog box.

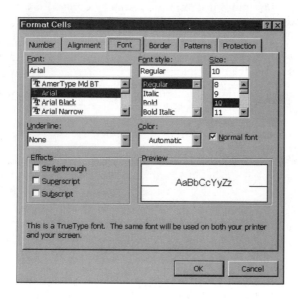

4. Make the desired changes and click OK.

Notice that you also can change the font style (bold, italic), underlining, color, and effects (strikethrough, superscript, or subscript). If you click the check box labeled Normal font, Excel displays the selections for the font defined for the Normal style.

See also "Creating and modifying named styles," in this part.

Changing row height

Row height is measured in *points* (a standard unit of measurement in the printing trade; 72 points equal one inch). Changing the row height is useful for spacing out rows; it's better to change the row height than to insert empty rows between rows of data. If you want, you can select several rows before using the following techniques to set row height:

- ✦ Drag the lower row border with the mouse until the row is the desired height.

- ✦ Choose the Format⇨Row⇨Height command and enter a value (in points) in the Row Height dialog box.

- ✦ Double-click the bottom border of a row to automatically set the row height to the tallest entry in the row. You also can use the Format⇨Row⇨AutoFit command for this.

Remember: The default row height depends on the font defined in the Normal style. Excel adjusts row heights automatically to accommodate the tallest font in the row. So, if you change the font size of a cell to, say, 20 points, Excel makes the row taller so that the entire text is visible.

See also "Creating and modifying named styles," in this part.

Changing text attributes

The easiest way to change text attributes (bold, italic, underline, and strikethrough) is to select the cell or range and then click the appropriate tool on the Formatting toolbar (for Bold, Italic, or Underline).

Or you can use the following shortcut keys to modify the selected cells.

Format	Shortcut Keys
B Bold	Ctrl+B
I Italic	Ctrl+I
U Underline	Ctrl+U
~~Strikethrough~~	Ctrl+5

These toolbar buttons and shortcut keys act as a toggle. For example, you can turn bold on and off by repeatedly pressing Ctrl+B (or clicking the Bold tool).

See also "Adding borders to a cell or range," in this part.

Changing text orientation (direction)

Normally, the contents of a cell are displayed horizontally. In some cases you may want to display the text vertically or at an angle.

	2nd Q.	Unit-1	Unit-2	Unit-3		
3						
4	January	132	232	546		
5	February	154	209	566		
6	March	165	312	433		
7						
8						
9						
10						
11						
12						

1. Select the cell or range to modify.

2. Choose the Format➪Cells command (or press Ctrl+1).

3. Click the Alignment tab in the Format Cells dialog box.

4. Select one of the options in the Orientation section.

Adjust the angle by dragging the gauge or specifying an angle (in degrees). Vertical text is represented by an angle of 90 degrees (text rotated upwards) or – 90 degrees (text rotated downwards).

5. Click OK to apply the formatting to the selection.

To quickly rotate text downwards, select the text and click the vertical box labeled "Text".

Remember: Excel adjusts the row height in order to display the text. If this is not desirable, you can use the merge cells feature to avoid having a larger row height.

See also "Merging cells," in this part.

Copying formats

The quickest way to copy the formats from one cell to another cell or range is to use the Format Painter button on the Standard toolbar:

1. Select the cell or range that has the formatting attributes that you want to copy.

 2. Click the Format Painter button.

Notice that the mouse pointer appears as a miniature paintbrush.

3. Select (paint) the cells to which you want to apply the formats.

4. Release the mouse button, and Excel copies the formats.

Double-clicking the Format Painter button causes the mouse pointer to remain a paintbrush after you release the mouse button. This lets you paint other areas of the worksheet with the same formats. To exit paint mode, click the Format Painter button again (or press Esc).

Following is another way to copy formats:

1. Select the cell or range that has the formatting attributes that you want to copy.

2. Choose the Edit⇨Copy command.

3. Select the cell or range to which you want to apply the formats.

4. Choose the Edit⇨Paste Special command, click the Formats option, and click OK.

Creating custom number formats

Excel provides you with quite a few predefined number formats. If none of these is satisfactory, you need to create a custom number format.

1. Select the cell or range of cells that contains the values to format.

2. Choose the Format⇨Cells command (or press Ctrl+1).

3. Click the Number tab in the Format Cells dialog box.

4. Select the Custom category.

5. Construct a number format by specifying a series of codes in the Type field.

6. Click OK to store the custom number format and apply it to the selected cells.

The custom number format is now available for you to use with other cells.

The formatting codes available for custom number formats, date, and time are described in the Excel online help. To see some examples of formatting codes, click the Custom category in the Number tab of the Format Cells dialog box.

Remember: Custom number formats are stored with the workbook. To make the custom format available in a different workbook, you must copy a cell that uses the custom format to the other workbook.

Creating and modifying named styles

A named style can consist of settings for six different attributes. However, a style doesn't have to use *all* of the attributes. The attributes that make up a style are as follows:

✦ Number format

✦ Font (type, size, and color)

✦ Alignment (vertical and horizontal)

✦ Borders

✦ Pattern

✦ Protection (locked and hidden)

The easiest way to create a style is "by example." This means that you format a cell to have the style characteristics that you want and then let Excel create the style from that cell. To create a style by example, do the following:

1. Select a cell and apply the formatting that will make up the style.

2. Choose the Format⇨Style command.

Excel displays its Style dialog box.

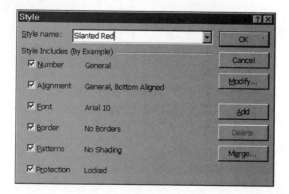

3. Enter a name for the style in the Style name drop-down box.

4. Remove the check marks from any of the six attributes that you don't want to be part of the style (optional).

5. Click OK to create the style.

The new style is available and you can apply it to other cells or ranges.

See also "Applying named styles," "Changing fonts and text sizes," and "Changing row height," in this part.

Formatting numbers

Excel is smart enough to perform some number formatting for you automatically. For example, if you enter **9.6%** into a cell, Excel knows that you want to use a percentage format and applies it for you automatically. Similarly, if you use commas to separate thousands (such as **123,456**), or a dollar sign to indicate currency (such as **$123.45**), Excel applies appropriate formatting for you.

Use the Formatting toolbar to quickly apply common number formats. When you click one of these buttons, the active cell takes on the specified number format. The following table lists these toolbar buttons.

Button Name	Formatting Applied
Currency Style	Adds a dollar sign to the left, separates thousands with a comma, and displays the value with two digits to the right of the decimal point
Percent Style	Displays the value as a percentage with no decimal places
Comma Style	Separates thousands with a comma and displays the value with two digits to the right of the decimal place
Increase Decimal	Increases the number of digits to the right of the decimal point by one
Decrease Decimal	Decreases the number of digits to the right of the decimal point by one

Remember: These five toolbar buttons actually apply predefined *styles* to the selected cells. This is not the same as simply changing the number format.

If none of the predefined number formats fits the bill, you need to use the Format Cells dialog box:

1. Select the cell or range that contains the values to format.

2. Choose the Format⇨Cells command (or press Ctrl+1).

3. Click the Number tab.

4. Select one of the 12 categories of number formats.

When you select a category from the list box, the right side of the panel changes to display appropriate options.

5. Select an option from the right side of the dialog box.

Options will vary, depending on your category choice. The top of the panel displays a sample of how the active cell will appear with the selected number format.

6. After you make your choices, click OK to apply the number format to all of the selected cells.

Remember: If the cell displays a series of pound signs (such as ####), it means that the column is not wide enough to display the value using the number format that you selected. The solution is to make the column wider or change the number format as described in "Changing column width," in this part.

Formatting selected characters in a cell

If a cell contains text, Excel lets you format individual characters in the cell. For example, you can make the first letter of the cell appear in a larger typeface (font).

To format only part of a cell, follow these steps:

1. Select the cell that contains the characters you want to format.

2. Get into cell edit mode (press F2, or double-click the cell).

3. Select the characters that you want to format. You can select characters by dragging the mouse over them or by holding down Shift as you press the left- or right-arrow key.

4. Use any of the standard formatting techniques: toolbar buttons, the Format Cells dialog box, or shortcut keys to modify the text.

5. Press Enter.

The changes apply only to the selected characters in the cell.

Remember: This technique works only with cells that contain text — it doesn't work with cells that contain values or formulas.

If you want to apply character formatting to a value, format the value as Text using the Number panel of the Format Cells dialog box. Then you can apply individual character formatting to the cell contents.

Formatting based on a cell's contents

When you use conditional formatting, Excel automatically changes the formatting of a cell depending on the value in the cell. For example, you may want to visually identify all cells in a range that exceed a certain value. You can specify up to three conditions for a cell:

1. Select the cell or range that you want to format conditionally.

2. Choose the Format➪Conditional Formatting command.

3. In the box in the upper-left corner of the Conditional Formatting dialog box, specify whether to base formatting on the cell's value (Cell Value Is) or the value of a formula in a different cell (Formula Is).

4. If the condition is based on the cell's value, specify the condition (for example, Cell Value Is greater than 100). If the condition is based on a formula, enter the address that holds the formula (the formula must evaluate to either True or False).

5. Click the Format button and specify the formatting that you want to apply if the condition is true.

6. If you want to specify additional conditions for the selected cells, click the Add button and repeat Steps 3 through 5 (the dialog box will expand). You can specify up to three conditions.

If the cell doesn't meet the condition (or conditions) you specified, it takes on the standard formatting for the cell.

When you copy a cell that has conditional formatting, the conditional formatting applies to all copies.

Hiding cells

You can "hide" the contents of a cell in several ways:

✦ Apply a custom number format consisting of three semicolons (;;;).

✦ Make the text color the same as the background color.

✦ Cover the cell with an object.

All three of these techniques have the same flaw: When the cell pointer is on the cell, its contents can be seen in the formula bar. If you want to avoid this and make the cell contents truly invisible, follow these steps:

1. Select the cell or range and make the text color the same as the background color.

2. Choose Format➪Cells (or press Ctrl+1).

3. Click the Protection tab.

4. Check the Hidden check box.

5. Click OK.

6. Select the Tools➪Protection➪Protect Sheet command to turn on the Hidden attribute for the selected cells.

See also "Protecting a Worksheet," in Part II.

Remember: You aren't able to make any changes when the worksheet is protected.

Hiding columns and rows

Hiding columns and rows is useful if you don't want users to see particular information or if you don't want some information to print.

To hide a column(s) or row(s):

1. Select the column(s) or row(s) that you want to hide.

2. Choose Format➪Column➪Hide or Format➪Row➪Hide.

You also can drag a column's right border to the left or a row's bottom border upward to hide it.

Remember: A hidden column or row has a width or height of 0.
When you use the arrow keys to move the cell pointer, cells in
hidden columns or rows are skipped. In other words, you can't use
the arrow keys to move to a cell in a hidden row or column.

See also "Unhiding rows or columns," in this part.

Indenting the contents of a cell

Excel enables you to indent text in a cell. Using this feature is
much easier than padding the cell with spaces to indent. The
following figure shows six cells that are indented.

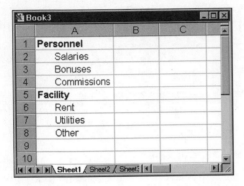

1. Select the cell or range of cells to indent.

2. Choose the Format⇨Cells command (or press Ctrl+1).

3. Click the Alignment tab in the Format Cells dialog box.

4. Specify the number of spaces to indent in the Indent text box.

5. Click OK.

Indented text is always left-aligned.

Justifying (refitting) text across cells

Justifying text redistributes the text in cells so that it fits into a
specified range. You can make the text either wider (so it uses
fewer rows) or narrower (so that it uses more rows).

The following figure shows a range of text before and after being
redistributed to fit a specified range.

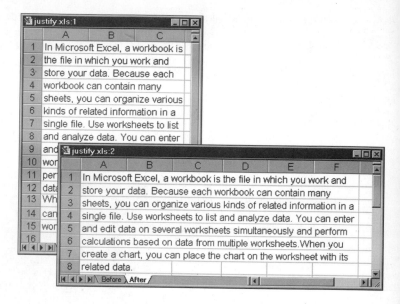

To justify text across cells, follow these steps:

1. Select the text to be justified.

The text must be in cells in a single column. Blank rows serve as paragraph markers.

2. Extend the selection to the right so that the selection is as wide as you want the end result to be.

3. Choose the Edit⇨Fill⇨Justify command.

Excel redistributes the text so that it fits in the selected range.

If the range you select isn't large enough to hold all of the text, Excel warns you and allows you to continue or abort. Be careful: justified text overwrites anything that gets in its way.

Remember: In all cases, the text must be in a single column of cells. After you justify the text, it remains in a single column.

Merging cells

Excel offers a helpful feature that allows you to merge cells into a single, larger cell. This feature lets you have cells of unequal sizes. For example, if you have a table that spans six columns, you can merge six cells at the top to form a single larger cell for the table's title. In the following figure, cells C3:E3 are merged horizontally, and cells A5:A8 are merged vertically.

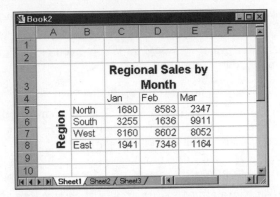

+ You can merge cells horizontally or vertically.

+ When a selection contains more than one non-empty cell, the merged cells contain the contents and formatting of the upper-left cell of the merged range.

+ It's important to understand that *cells* get merged — not the *contents* of cells. When you merge cells, you receive a warning if the selected range contains more than one non-empty cell.

To merge a range of cells:

1. Select the cells to be merged.

2. Choose Format⇨Cells (or press Ctrl+1).

3. Click the Alignment tab.

4. Select the Merge cells check box.

5. Click OK.

 You can also merge cells by using the Merge and Center button on the Formatting toolbar. To "unmerge" cells, clear the Merge cells check box in the Alignment tab of the Format Cells dialog box.

Unhiding rows or columns

Unhiding a hidden row or column can be a bit tricky because you can't directly select a row or column that's hidden. Here's how:

1. Choose Edit⇨Go To (or its F5 equivalent) to have Excel display its Go To dialog box.

2. In the Reference field, enter a cell address that's in the hidden row or column.

For example, if you want to unhide row 1, enter **A1** (or any other cell address in row 1).

3. Choose the Format⇨Row⇨Unhide command or the Format⇨Column⇨Unhide command.

See also "Hiding columns and rows," in this part.

To unhide all hidden columns or rows, select the entire worksheet (Ctrl+A), and then select the Format⇨Row⇨Unhide command or the Format⇨Column⇨Unhide command.

Using AutoFormats

The Excel AutoFormatting feature applies attractive formatting to a table automatically.

To apply an AutoFormat, follow these steps:

1. Move the cell pointer anywhere within a table that you want to format (Excel determines the table's boundaries automatically).

2. Choose the Format⇨AutoFormat command.

Excel responds with its AutoFormat dialog box.

3. Select one of the 17 AutoFormats from the list and click OK.

Excel formats the table using the selected AutoFormat.

You can't define your own AutoFormats, but you *can* control the type of formatting that is applied. When you click the Options button in the AutoFormat dialog box, the dialog box expands to show six options.

Initially, the six check boxes are all checked, which means that Excel applies formatting from all six categories. If you want it to skip one or more categories, just uncheck the appropriate boxes by clicking in them before you click OK.

Wrapping text within a cell

Wrapping text within a cell is a good way to display more information without making the column wider. This is useful for lengthy table headings, as shown in the following figure.

Book4						
	A	B	C	D	E	F
1						
2		Projected Sales	Actual Sales	Actual Minus Projected		
3	Chairs	244	211	-33		
4	Tables	45	55	10		
5	Desks	17	15	-2		
6	Lamps	24	32	8		
7		330	313	-17		
8						
9						

Sheet1 \ Sheet2 / Sheet3 /

To format a cell or range so that the words wrap around, follow these steps:

1. Select the cell or range that you want to apply word wrap formatting to.

2. Choose Format⇨Cells (or press Ctrl+1).

3. Click the Alignment tab of the Format Cells dialog box.

4. Check the box labeled <u>W</u>rap text.

5. Click OK to apply the formatting to the selection.

Remember: When you decrease the column width of a cell that's formatted with wrap text, the words wrap around to the next line to accommodate the new column width.

Outlining Your Worksheet

Some types of worksheets may benefit from an outline. An outline enables you to display hierarchical information at different levels of detail.

Creating an outline automatically

In most cases, you should let Excel create the outline for you. Excel can do the job in a few seconds, whereas you may take ten minutes or more.

To have Excel create an outline, follow these steps:

1. Move the cell pointer anywhere within the range of data that you're outlining.

2. Choose <u>D</u>ata⇨Group and Outline⇨<u>A</u>uto Outline.

Excel analyzes the formulas in the range and creates the outline. Depending on the formulas you have, Excel creates a row outline, a column outline, or both.

	A	B	C	D	E	I	
1	State	Jan	Feb	Mar	Q1 Total	Q2 Total	Q:
2	California	1118	1960	1252	4330	4507	
3	Washington	1247	1238	1028	3513	4703	
4	Oregon	1460	1954	1726	5140	4369	
5	Nevada	1345	1375	1075	3795	4663	
6	**West Total**	**5170**	**6527**	**5081**	**16778**	**18242**	
7	New York	1429	1316	1993	4738	4763	
8	New Jersey	1735	1406	1224	4365	4316	
9	Massachusetts	1099	1233	1110	3442	4155	
10	Florida	1705	1792	1225	4722	4630	
11	**East Total**	**5968**	**5747**	**5552**	**17267**	**17864**	
17	**Central Total**	**7441**	**6920**	**6664**	**21025**	**20805**	
18	**Grand Total**	**18579**	**19194**	**17297**	**55070**	**56911**	
19							

Remember: A worksheet can have only one outline. If the worksheet already has an outline, Excel asks whether you want to modify the existing outline. Click OK to force Excel to remove the old outline and create a new one.

See also "Determining whether a worksheet is suitable for an outline," in this part.

Creating an outline manually

Usually, letting Excel create the outline is the best approach. If the outline that Excel creates isn't what you had in mind, however, you can create one manually.

You must create an outline manually when:

✦ The summary rows aren't consistent (some formulas are above the data and some are below the data).

✦ The range doesn't contain any formulas. Because Excel uses the formulas to determine how to create the outline, it is not able to make an outline if there are no formulas.

Creating an outline manually consists of creating groups of rows (for row outlines) or groups of columns (for column outlines).

To create a group of rows, follow these steps:

1. Select the entire row or rows that you want to be included in the group — but do *not* select the row that has the summary formulas.

2. Choose <u>D</u>ata⇨<u>G</u>roup and Outline⇨<u>G</u>roup. Excel displays the outline symbols for the group as it's created.

3. Repeat Steps 1 and 2 for each group that you want to create.

When you collapse the outline (that is, show less detail), rows in the group are hidden. But the summary row, which is not in the group, isn't hidden.

Follow the same steps to create a group of columns — but select columns instead of rows.

If you group the wrong rows or columns, you can ungroup the group with the <u>D</u>ata⇨<u>G</u>roup and Outline⇨<u>U</u>ngroup command. (You must select the grouped rows or columns before using the Ungroup command.)

Remember: You can also select groups of groups to create multi-level outlines. When creating multilevel outlines, always start with the "innermost" groupings and then work your way out.

See also "Determining whether a worksheet is suitable for an outline," in this part.

Determining whether a worksheet is suitable for an outline

Before you create an outline, you need to ensure that:

+ The data is appropriate for an outline.

+ The formulas are set up properly.

Generally, the data should be arranged in a hierarchy. An example of hierarchical data is a budget that consists of an arrangement such as the following:

Division

Department

Budget Category

Budget Item

In this case, each budget item (for example, airfare and hotel expenses) is part of a budget category (for example, travel expenses). Each department has its own budget, and the departments are rolled up into divisions. This type of arrangement is well suited for a row outline.

Before creating an outline, make sure that you enter summary formulas in the same relative location. Generally, formulas that compute summary formulas (such as subtotals) are entered below the data to which they refer. In some cases, however, the summary formulas are entered above the referenced cells.

If your summary formulas aren't consistent (that is, some are above and some are below the data), automatic outlining won't produce the results you want. You still can create an outline, but you must do it manually.

See also "Creating an outline automatically" and "Creating an outline manually," both in this part.

Expanding and contracting an outline

To display various levels of detail in a worksheet outline, click the appropriate outline symbol at the left side of the screen (for row outlines) or the top of the screen (for column outlines).

Number symbols (1,2,3, and so on)	Displays a level corresponding to the number. Clicking the 1 button collapses the outline as small as it will go (less detail). Clicking the 2 button expands the outline to show one level of detail, and so on. Choosing a level number displays the detail for that level, plus any lower levels. To display all of the detail, click the highest level number.
Plus (+) or minus (−) symbols	Expands (+) or collapses (−) a particular section of the outline.

If you prefer, you can use the Hide Detail and Show Detail commands on the Data⇨Group and Outline menu to hide and show details.

If you find yourself constantly adjusting the outline to show different reports, consider creating custom views. A Custom view enables you to save a particular view and give it a name. To create a custom view, select the View⇨Custom Views command and click the Add button in the Custom Views dialog box. A custom view can include print settings, hidden rows, hidden columns, and filter settings.

See also "Creating and using named views," in Part II.

Hiding outline symbols

The symbols displayed when a worksheet outline is present can take up quite a bit of screen space. If you want to see as much of the data as possible on-screen, you can temporarily hide these symbols without removing the outline. To do so, press Ctrl+8. (Ctrl+8 is a toggle. Press Ctrl+8 to bring back the symbols.)

Remember: When you hide the outline symbols, the outline is still in effect and the worksheet displays the data at the current outline level. That is, some rows or columns may be hidden.

If you use the View Manager to save named views of your outline, the status of the outline symbols is also saved as part of the view. This enables you to name some views with the outline symbols and other views without them.

Removing an outline

If you decide that you no longer need an outline, you can remove it (the data remains, but the outline goes away). Just select the Data⇨Group and Outline⇨Clear Outline command. The outline is fully expanded (all hidden rows and columns are unhidden), and the outline symbols disappear.

Removing an outline can't be undone, so make sure that you really want to remove the outline before selecting this command.

Printing Your Work

Clicking the Print button on the Standard toolbar is a quick way to print the current worksheet using the default settings. If you've changed any of the default print settings, Excel uses the settings you put in; otherwise, it uses these default settings:

- ✦ Prints the active worksheet (or all selected worksheets), including any embedded charts or drawing objects
- ✦ Prints one copy
- ✦ Prints the entire worksheet (by default, Excel prints all active worksheets)
- ✦ Prints in portrait mode
- ✦ Doesn't scale the printed output
- ✦ Uses 1-inch margins for the top and bottom and $3/4$-inch margins for the left and right
- ✦ Doesn't print a header or footer
- ✦ For wide worksheets that span multiple pages it prints down and then over

Adjusting margins

A *margin* is the blank space on the side of the printed page. The wider the margins, the less space is available for printing. You can control all four page margins from Excel.

To adjust margins, follow these steps:

1. Select the File⇔Page Setup command.

2. Click the Margins tab in the Page Setup dialog box.

3. Click the appropriate spinner to change the margin value (or you can enter a value directly).

In addition to the page margins, you can adjust the distance of the header from the top of the page and the distance of the footer from the bottom of the page. These settings should be less than the corresponding margin; otherwise, the header or footer may overlap with the printed output.

You also can change the margins while you're previewing your output — ideal for last-minute adjustments before printing.

See also "Previewing your work," in this part.

Remember: The page preview box in the Margins tab of the Page Setup dialog box is a bit deceiving because it doesn't really show you how your changes look in relation to the page. Rather, it simply displays a darker line to let you know which of the margins you're adjusting.

Centering printed output

Normally, Excel prints a page at the top and left margins. If you want the output to be centered vertically or horizontally on the page, follow these steps:

1. Select the File⇔Page Setup command.

2. Click the Margins tab of the Page Setup dialog box.

3. Check the appropriate check boxes in the Center on page section: Horizontally or Vertically.

4. Click OK to close the Page Setup dialog box.

Changing default printing settings with a template

If you find that you're never satisfied with the Excel default print settings, you may want to create a template with the print settings that you use most often.

1. Start with an empty workbook.

2. Adjust the print settings to your liking.

3. Save the workbook as a template in your Excel\XLStart folder or in the Office\XLStart folder (or in Microsoft Office\Office\ XLStart), using the name **Book.xlt**.

Excel uses this template as the basis for all new workbooks, and your custom print settings become the default settings.

Changing the header or footer

A *header* is information that appears at the top of each printed page. A *footer* is information that appears at the bottom of each printed page.

Headers and footers each have three sections: left, center, and right. For example, you can specify a header that consists of your name left-justified, the worksheet name centered, and the page number right-justified.

Remember: In Excel, the default is no header or footer.

To specify a header or footer, follow these steps:

1. Select the File⇨Page Setup command.

2. Click the Header/Footer tab of the Page Setup dialog box.

3. Select a pre-defined header or footer from the Header or Footer drop-down list.

If none of the pre-defined headers or footers is what you want, you need to define a customized header or footer:

1. Click the Custom Header or Custom Footer button in the Header/Footer tab of the Page Setup dialog box.

Excel displays a new dialog box.

2. Enter the desired information in any or all of the three sections. Or click any of the seven buttons (described in the following table) to enter a special code.

Button	*Code*	*Function*
Font	Not applicable	Lets you choose a font for the selected text
Page Number	&[Page]	Inserts the page number
Total Pages	&[Pages]	Inserts the total number of pages to be printed
Date	&[Date]	Inserts the current date
Time	&[Time]	Inserts the current time
File Name	&[File]	Inserts the workbook name
Sheet Name	&[Tab]	Inserts the sheet's name

3. Click OK to close the Header (or Footer) dialog box and then click OK to close the Page Setup dialog box.

You can combine text and codes and insert as many codes as you like into each section. If the text you enter uses an ampersand (&), you must enter it twice (because an ampersand is used by Excel to signal a code). For example, to enter the text *Research & Development* into a section of a header or footer, type **Research && Development.**

You can use as many lines as you like. Press Enter to force a line break for multiline headers or footers.

Changing page orientation

To change the page orientation (landscape or portrait) of your printed output, follow these steps:

1. Select the File⇨Page Setup command.

2. Click the Page tab of the Page Setup dialog box.

3. Select either Portrait (tall pages) or Landscape (wide pages).

Use landscape orientation if you have a wide range that doesn't fit on a vertically oriented page.

Inserting manual page breaks

Excel handles page breaks automatically. After you print or preview your worksheet, it displays dashed lines to indicate where page breaks will occur. Sometimes, you want to force a page break — either a vertical or a horizontal one.

To insert a horizontal manual page break, follow these steps:

1. Move the cell pointer to the cell that will begin the new page, but make sure that it's in column A (otherwise, you'll insert a vertical page break and a horizontal page break).

2. Choose Insert⇨Page Break to create the page break.

The page break is inserted in the row above the cell pointer.

To insert a vertical page break, follow these steps:

1. Move the cell pointer to the cell that will begin the new page, but make sure that it's in row 1 (otherwise, you'll insert a horizontal page break and a vertical page break).

2. Select Insert⇨Page Break to create the page break.

The page break is inserted in the column to the left of the cell pointer.

When manipulating page breaks, it's often helpful to use the zoom feature to zoom out. This gives you a bird's-eye view of the worksheet, and you can see more pages at once. *See also* "Zooming worksheets," in Part II.

Previewing and adjusting page breaks

Excel offers the Page Break Preview viewing mode. The View⇨ Page Break Preview command displays your worksheet in a way that lets you move the page breaks by dragging them with your mouse. This view doesn't show a true page preview (for example, it doesn't show headers and footers). Rather, it's an easy way to make sure the pages break at desired locations.

✦ Excel automatically zooms out, so you can see more on the screen. You can set the zoom factor to whatever you like.

✦ If you've specified a print area (rather than the entire worksheet), the print area appears in white and all of the other cells are in a darker color.

✦ Change a page break by dragging it.

✦ While you're previewing the page breaks, you have full access to all of the Excel commands. To return to normal viewing, use the View⇨Normal command.

Previewing your work

The Excel print preview feature shows an image of the printed output on your screen — a handy feature that saves time and paper.

There are several ways to access the print preview feature:

✦ Select the File⇨Print Preview command.

✦ Click the Print Preview button on the Standard toolbar. Or you can press Shift and click the Print button on the Standard toolbar (the Print button serves a dual purpose).

✦ Click the Preview button in the Print dialog box.

✦ Click the Print Preview button in the Page Setup dialog box.

Any of these methods changes the Excel window to a special preview window. The preview window has several buttons along the top, the most important of which is Margins. Clicking it displays adjustable column and margin markers. You can drag the column or margin markers to make changes that appear on-screen.

Printing cell comments

If one or more cells in your worksheet has a cell comment, you can print these comments along with the worksheet:

1. Select File⇨Page Setup.

2. Click the Sheet tab in the Page Setup dialog box.

3. In the Comments drop-down box, choose one of the following:

- **(None):** Comments won't be printed.

- **At end of sheet:** All comments will be printed at the end of the printout, beginning on a new sheet.

- **As displayed on sheet:** Comments are printed exactly as they appear. Only visible comments will be printed.

Printing colors in black and white

If you have a colorful worksheet, but your printer is stuck in a monochrome world, you may discover that the worksheet colors don't translate well to black and white. In this case, you need to instruct Excel to ignore the colors when printing:

1. Select File⇨Page Setup.

2. Click the Sheet tab of the Page Setup dialog box.

3. Place a check mark next to the Black and white check box.

See also "Applying background colors and patterns," in this part.

Printing in draft quality

Printing in draft mode doesn't print embedded charts or drawing objects, cell gridlines, or borders. This usually reduces the printing time and is handy for getting a quick printout.

To print your work in draft mode, follow these steps:

1. Select File⇨Page Setup.

2. Click the Sheet tab of the Page Setup dialog box.

3. Place a check mark next to the Draft quality check box.

Printing noncontiguous ranges

Excel enables you to specify a print area that consists of noncontiguous ranges (a multiple selection). To do so, follow these steps:

1. Press Ctrl while you select the ranges.

2. Choose File⇨Print.

3. Select the Selection option.

This is a handy feature, but you may not like the fact that Excel prints each range on a new sheet of paper.

One solution to this problem is to create live "snapshots" of the ranges and paste these snapshots to an empty area of the worksheet. Then you can print this new area that consists of the snapshots and Excel doesn't skip to a new page for each range.

To create a live snapshot of a range, follow these steps:

1. Select the range and copy it to the Clipboard.

2. Activate the cell where you want to paste the snapshot (an empty worksheet is a good choice).

3. Press the Shift key and choose Edit⇨Paste Picture Link to paste a live link.

4. Repeat Steps 1 through 3 for the other ranges you want to print.

5. Arrange the snapshots by dragging them.

6. Select the range that holds the snapshot and print only that range.

Printing or suppressing gridlines

To change the way Excel handles worksheet gridlines when printing, follow these steps:

1. Select the File⇨Page Setup command.

2. Click the Sheet tab of the Page Setup dialog box.

3. Place a check mark in the Gridlines check box to print gridlines; remove the check to suppress gridline printing.

Printing row and column headings

If you want to make it easy to identify specific cell addresses from a printout, you'll want to print the row and column headings. To do so, follow these steps:

1. Select the File⇨Page Setup command.

2. Click the Sheet tab of the Page Setup dialog box.

3. Place a check mark in the Row and column headings check box.

Printing selected pages

If your printed output uses multiple pages, you may not always want to print all of the pages. To select a range of pages to print, follow these steps:

1. Select the File⇨Print command.

2. In the Print range section of the Print dialog box, indicate the number of the first and last pages to print. You can use the spinner controls, or you can type the page numbers in the edit boxes.

Removing manual page breaks

To remove a manual page break, follow these steps:

1. Move the cell pointer anywhere in the first row beneath a horizontal page break or the first column to the right of a vertical page break.

2. Select the Insert⇨Remove Page Break command.

To remove all manual page breaks in the worksheet, click the Select All button (or press Ctrl+A); then choose the Insert⇨Reset All Page Breaks command.

Scaling your printed output

To scale your printed output, follow these steps:

1. Select File⇨Page Setup.

2. Click the Page tab of the Page Setup dialog box.

3. Enter a scaling factor manually in the % Normal Size box, or let Excel scale the output automatically to fit on the desired number of pages.

If you want to return to normal scaling, enter **100** in the box labeled % Normal Size.

Selecting a printer

If you have access to more than one printer, you may need to select the correct printer before printing. To do so, follow these steps:

1. Select File⇨Print.

2. In the Print dialog box, select the printer from the drop-down list labeled Name.

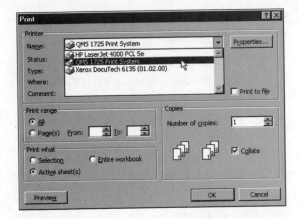

The Print dialog box also lists information about the selected printer, such as its status and where it's connected.

Selecting paper size

To change the paper size of the printed output, follow these steps:

1. Select the File⇨Page Setup command.

2. Click the Page tab of the Page Setup dialog box.

3. Select the paper size from the list labeled Paper size.

Setting the print area

To specify a particular range to print, follow these steps:

1. Select the range that you want to print. Press Ctrl to select nonadjacent ranges.

2. Choose the File⇨Print Area⇨Set Print Area command.

You can use the following steps to print only a specific range:

1. Select a range of cells.

2. Choose the File⇨Print command.

3. Choose the Selection option in the Print dialog box.

Setting print titles

Many worksheets are set up with titles in the first row and descriptive names in the first column. If such a worksheet requires more than one page to print, you may find it difficult to read subsequent pages because the text in the first row and first column won't be printed. Excel offers a simple solution: print titles.

To specify print titles, follow these steps:

1. Select the File⇨Page Setup command.

2. Click the Sheet tab of the Page Setup dialog box.

3. Activate the appropriate box in the Print Titles section and select the rows or columns in the worksheet.

Or you can enter these references manually. For example, to specify rows 1 and 2 as repeating rows, enter **1:2**.

Remember: Don't confuse print titles with headers; these are two different concepts. Headers appear at the top of each page and contain information such as the worksheet name, date, or page number. Print titles describe the data being printed, such as field names in a database table or list.

You can specify different print titles for each worksheet in the workbook. Excel remembers print titles by creating sheet-level names (Print_Titles).

Specifying the beginning page number

If your printed output will be inserted into another report, you may want to specify a beginning page number so the pages collate correctly when inserted into the report. To do so, follow these steps:

1. Select the File⇨Page Setup command.

2. Click the Page tab of the Page Setup dialog box.

3. Specify a page number for the first page in the First page number text box.

Specifying what to print

Excel gives you several options when you decide to print. To tell Excel what to print, follow these steps:

1. Select the File⇨Print command.

2. In the Print what section of the Print dialog box, specify what to print. You have three options:

• Selection: Prints only the range that you selected before issuing the File⇨Print command.

• Active sheet(s): Prints the active sheet or all sheets that you selected. You can select multiple sheets by pressing Ctrl and clicking the sheet tabs. If multiple sheets are selected, each sheet begins printing on a new page.

- **Entire workbook:** Prints the entire workbook, including chart sheets, dialog sheets, and VBA modules.

Remember: If you choose the Active sheet(s) option, Excel prints the entire sheet — or just the range named Print_Area. Each worksheet can have a range named Print_Area. You can set the print area by selecting it and then choosing the File⇨Print Area⇨ Set Print Area command. This is a standard named range, so you can edit the range's reference manually if you like.

Spell checking

Excel has a spell checker that works just like the feature found in word processing programs. You can access the spell checker using any of these methods:

◆ Select the Tools⇨Spelling command.

 ◆ Click the Spelling button on the Standard toolbar.

◆ Press F7.

The extent of the spell checking depends on what was selected when you accessed the dialog box.

What Is Selected	What Gets Checked
A single cell	The entire worksheet, including cell contents, notes, text in graphic objects and charts, and page headers and footers
A range of cells	Only that range is checked
A group of characters	Only those characters are checked in the formula bar

If Excel encounters a word that isn't in the current dictionary or is misspelled, it offers a list of suggestions you can click to respond to.

Part IV

Entering and Editing Worksheet Data

This part deals with two general topics of Microsoft Excel 2000: entering data into worksheet cells and editing (or changing) the data after you enter it.

In this part . . .

- ✓ Entering data into cells
- ✓ Selecting cells and ranges
- ✓ Copying cells and ranges
- ✓ Editing the contents of a cell
- ✓ Moving cells and ranges
- ✓ Erasing cells and ranges
- ✓ Searching and replacing data
- ✓ Undoing changes and mistakes

Copying Cells and Ranges

Copying cells is a very common spreadsheet operation, and several types of copying are allowed. You can do any of the following:

✦ Copy one cell to another cell.

✦ Copy a cell to a range of cells. The source cell is copied to every cell in the destination range.

✦ Copy a range to another range.

Older versions of Excel use the Windows Clipboard to hold data for copying and pasting. The Windows Clipboard can store only one piece of data at a time. When you copy new data to the Windows Clipboard, it replaces the existing data.

Excel 2000 uses the new Office Clipboard, which can store up to 12 data items at one time. You can use the new Office Clipboard to cut and paste between Excel 2000 and other Office 2000 applications, such as Word and PowerPoint.

Remember: Copying a cell normally copies the cell contents, its cell comment (if any), and the formatting applied to the original cell. When you copy a cell that contains a formula, the cell references in the copied formulas are changed automatically to be relative to their new location.

See also "Using Cell Comments," in this part.

In general, copying consists of two steps:

1. Select the cell or range to copy (the source range) and copy it to the Office Clipboard.

2. Move the cell pointer to the range that will hold the copy (the destination range) and paste the Clipboard contents.

You may select more than one cell or range to copy at a time. When you copy the second cell or range to the Office Clipboard, Excel pops up the Clipboard toolbar. From the Clipboard toolbar you can select an item to paste to a new range in your workbook or you can simultaneously paste all the copied items to the new range.

Copying a cell to another cell or a range

To copy the contents of one cell to a range of cells, follow these steps:

1. Move the cell pointer to the cell to copy.

2. Click the Copy button on the Standard toolbar (you can also press Ctrl+C or choose Edit⇨Copy).

3. Select the cell or range that you want to hold the copy.

4. Press Enter.

If the range that you're copying to is adjacent to the cell that you're copying from, you can drag the cell's AutoFill handle to copy it to the adjacent range.

Copying data as a picture

In some situations, you may want to copy a cell or range as a picture. Doing so creates a graphic object that's an exact duplicate of the copied range.

To copy data as a picture, follow these steps:

1. Select the cell or range.

2. Click the Copy button on the Standard toolbar (you can also press Ctrl+C or choose the Edit⇨Copy command).

3. Activate the cell or range where you want to paste the picture.

4. Press the Shift key and choose the Edit⇨Paste Picture command.

This procedure pastes a picture of the original cell or range. If you want the picture to be linked to the cell, press the Shift key and choose the Edit⇨Paste Picture Link command in Step 4. With a *linked* picture, any changes you make to the source range also appear in the picture.

You can manipulate the image qualities of the picture object using the Excel Picture toolbar (which appears automatically when you select a picture). For example, you can convert a color image to black and white.

Remember: The Edit⇨Paste Picture and the Edit⇨Paste Picture Link commands are available only if you press Shift while you click the Edit menu.

Copying data to another worksheet or workbook

To copy the contents of a cell or range to another worksheet or workbook, follow these steps:

1. Select the cell or range to copy.

 2. Click the Copy button on the Standard toolbar (you can also press Ctrl+C or choose the Edit⇨Copy command).

3. Click the tab of the worksheet that you're copying to.

If the worksheet is in a different workbook, activate that workbook (you can select the workbook from the Window menu) and then click the tab of the worksheet that you want to hold the copied data.

4. Select the upper-left cell of the range that you want to hold the copy.

5. Press Enter.

Copying formulas as values

Sometimes you may want to convert a formula to its current value:

1. Select the cell that contains the formula.

If you want to convert several formulas, you can select a range.

 2. Click the Copy button on the Standard toolbar (you can also press Ctrl+C or choose Edit⇨Copy).

3. Choose the Edit⇨Paste Special command.

4. In the Paste Special dialog box, select the Values option button.

5. Click OK.

6. Press Enter to cancel Copy mode.

Remember: The preceding procedure overwrites the formulas. If you want to put the current values of the formulas in a different area of the worksheet, select a different (blank) range before the preceding Step 3.

Copying a range to another range

To copy the contents of one range to another range of the same size, follow these steps:

1. Select the range to copy.

 2. Click the Copy button on the Standard toolbar (you can also press Ctrl+C or choose the Edit⇨Copy command).

3. Select the upper-left cell of the range that you want to hold the copy.

4. Press Enter.

If the location that you're copying to isn't too far away, you can follow these steps:

1. Select the cell or range to copy.

2. Hold down the Ctrl key.

3. Move the mouse pointer to any of the selection's borders.

The mouse pointer displays a small plus sign (+).

4. Drag the mouse to the location where you want to copy the cell or range.

5. Release the mouse button.

Excel copies the cell or range to the new location.

Remember: If the mouse pointer does not display a small plus sign (+) in Step 3, it means that the drag-and-drop feature is turned off. To turn the drag-and-drop feature on, follow these steps:

1. Select the Tools⇨Options command.

2. Click the Edit tab.

3. Check the check box labeled Allow cell drag and drop.

Editing a Cell's Contents

After you enter information into a cell, you can change it — or edit it. When you want to edit the contents of a cell, you can use one of these ways to get into cell edit mode:

✦ Double-click the cell to edit the cell contents directly in the cell.

✦ Press F2. This enables you to edit the cell contents directly in the cell.

✦ Activate the cell that you want to edit; then click in the formula bar to edit the cell contents in the formula bar.

✦ Activate the cell that you want to edit; then click the = icon in the formula bar to edit the cell contents in the formula bar.

All of these methods cause the formula bar to display two new mouse icons.

Icon	What It Does
X	Cancels editing, and the cell's contents aren't changed (Esc has the same effect)
Check Mark	Confirms the editing and enters the modified contents into the cell (Pressing Enter has the same effect)

Remember: If nothing happens when you double-click a cell, or if pressing F2 puts the cursor in the formula bar instead of the directly in the cell, the in-cell editing feature is turned off. To turn in-cell editing on, follow these steps:

1. Select the Tools⇨Options command.

2. Click the Edit tab.

3. Check the check box labeled Edit directly in cell.

When you're editing a cell that contains a formula, the Name box (located at the extreme left in the formula bar) displays a list of worksheet functions. You can select a function from the list and Excel provides assistance entering the arguments.

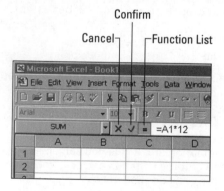

When you're editing the contents of a cell, the cursor changes to a vertical bar; you can move the vertical bar by using the direction keys. You can add new characters at the cursor location. Once you're in edit mode, you can use any of the following keys or key combinations to perform your edits:

✦ **Left/right arrow:** Moves the cursor left or right one character, respectively, without deleting any characters.

✦ **Ctrl+left/right arrow:** Moves the cursor one group of characters to the left or right, respectively.

✦ **Shift+left/right arrow:** Selects characters to the left or right of the cursor, respectively.

✦ **Shift+Home:** Selects from the cursor to the first character in the cell.

✦ **Shift+End:** Selects from the cursor to the last character in the cell.

✦ **Backspace:** Erases the character to the immediate left of the cursor.

✦ **Delete:** Erases the character to the right of the cursor or erases all selected characters.

✦ **Insert:** Places Excel in OVR (Overwrite) mode. Rather than add characters to the cell, you *overwrite,* or replace, existing characters with new ones, depending on the position of the cursor.

✦ **Home:** Moves the cursor to the beginning of the cell entry.

✦ **End:** Moves the cursor to the end of the cell entry.

✦ **Enter:** Accepts the edited data.

Remember: If you change your mind after editing a cell, you can select Edit➪Undo (or press Ctrl+Z) to restore the cell's previous contents.

You also can use the mouse to select characters while you're editing a cell. Just click and drag the mouse pointer over the characters that you want to select.

Remember: If the cell is locked and the worksheet is protected, you can't make any changes to the cell unless you unprotect the worksheet (with the Tools➪Protection➪Unprotect Sheet command).

See also "Protecting a Worksheet," in Part II.

Entering Data into a Worksheet

Each worksheet in a workbook is made up of cells, and a cell can hold any of four types of data:

✦ A value (including a date or a time)

✦ Text

✦ A logical value (TRUE or FALSE)

✦ A formula, which returns a value, text, or a logical value

Remember: An Excel worksheet can also hold charts, maps, drawings, diagrams, pictures, buttons, and other objects. These objects actually reside on the worksheet's *draw layer,* which is an invisible layer on top of each worksheet.

Entering the current date or time into a cell

If you need to date-stamp or time-stamp your worksheet, Excel provides two shortcut keys that do this for you:

✦ **Current date:** Ctrl+; (semicolon)

✦ **Current time:** Ctrl+Shift+; (semicolon)

Entering data into a specific range

If you're entering data into a range of cells, you may want to select the entire range of cells before you start entering data. This causes Excel to move the cell pointer to the next cell in the selection when you press Enter.

Here's how it works:

✦ If the selection consists of multiple rows, Excel moves down the column; when it reaches the end of the column, it moves to the top of the next column.

✦ To skip a cell, just press Enter without entering anything.

✦ To go backward, use Shift+Enter. If you prefer to enter the data by rows rather than by columns, use Tab rather than Enter.

Entering dates and times

To Excel, a date or a time is simply a value — but it's formatted to appear as a date or a time.

Excel's system for working with dates uses a serial number system. The earliest date that Excel understands is January 1, 1900 (which has a serial number of 1). January 2, 1900, has a serial number of 2, and so on. This system makes it easy to deal with dates in formulas.

Normally, you don't have to be concerned with the Excel serial number date system. You can simply enter a date in a familiar format, and Excel takes care of the details.

If you plan to use dates in formulas, make sure that the date you enter is actually recognized as a date (that is, a value); otherwise, your formulas will produce incorrect results. Excel is quite smart when it comes to recognizing dates that you enter into a cell, and it recognizes most common date formats. But it's not perfect. For example, Excel interprets the following entries as text, not dates:

✦ June 1 1998

✦ Jun-1 1998

✦ Jun-1/1998

TIP

The Year 2000 issue deserves a mention here. Entering 1/1/29 is interpreted by Excel as January 01, 2029. Entering 1/30 is interpreted by Excel as January 1930. To be safe, enter the year as a four-digit value, and then format it as desired.

Excel works with times by using fractional days. When working with times, you simply extend Excel's date serial number system to include decimals. For example, the date serial number for June 1, 1998, is 35947. Noon (halfway through the day) is represented internally as 35947.5.

The best way to deal with times is to enter the time into a cell in a recognized format. Here are some examples of time formats that Excel recognizes.

Entered into a Cell	Excel's Interpretation
11:30:00 am	11:30 a.m.
11:30:00 AM	11:30 a.m.
11:30 pm	11:30 p.m.
11:30	11:30 a.m.

You also can combine dates and times, as follows.

Entered into a Cell	Excel's Interpretation
6/1/98 11:30	11:30 a.m. on June 1, 1998

Entering formulas

A *formula* is a special type of cell entry that returns a result: When you enter a formula into a cell, the cell displays the result of the formula. The formula itself appears in the formula bar (which is just below the toolbars at the top of the Excel window) when the cell is activated.

A formula begins with an equal sign (=) and can consist of any of the following elements:

✦ Operators such as + (for addition) and * (for multiplication)

✦ Cell references, including addresses such as B4 or C12, as well as named cells and ranges

✦ Values and text

✦ Worksheet functions (such as SUM)

You can enter a formula into a cell in three ways: manually (typing it in), by pointing to cell references, or with the assistance of the formula palette. ***See also*** "Using Formulas," in Part V.

Entering formulas manually

To enter a formula manually, follow these steps:

1. Move the cell pointer to the cell that you want to hold the formula.

2. Type an equal sign (=) to signal the fact that the cell contains a formula.

3. Type the formula and press Enter.

As you type, the characters appear in the cell as well as in the formula bar. You can use all of the normal editing keys (Delete, Backspace, direction keys, and so on) when entering a formula.

Entering formulas by pointing

The pointing method of entering a formula still involves some manual typing. The advantage is that you don't have to type the cell or range references. Rather, you point to them in the worksheet, which is usually more accurate and less tedious.

The best way to explain this procedure is with an example. To enter the formula **=A1/A2** into cell A3 by the pointing method, just follow these steps:

1. Move the cell pointer to cell A3.

This is where you want the formula (and the result) to go.

2. Type an equal sign (=) to begin the formula.

3. Press the up arrow twice.

As you press this key, notice that Excel displays a faint moving border around the cell and that the cell reference appears in cell A3 and in the formula bar.

4. Type a division sign (/).

The faint border disappears, and Enter reappears in the status bar at the bottom of the screen.

5. Press the up arrow once.

A2 is added to the formula.

6. Press Enter to end the formula.

See also "Using Formulas" in Part V.

Entering fractions

To enter a fraction into a cell, leave a space between the whole number part and the fractional part. For example, to enter the decimal equivalent of 6 ⁷/₈, follow these steps:

1. Type **6**.

2. Type a space.

3. Type **7/8**.

4. Press Enter.

Excel enters 6.875 into the cell and automatically formats the cell as a fraction.

If there is no whole number part (for example, ¹/₈), you must enter a zero and a space first, like this: **0 1/8**.

Entering text into cells

To enter text (rather than a value or a formula) into a cell, follow these steps:

1. Move the cell pointer to the appropriate cell (this makes it the active cell).

2. Type the text.

3. Press Enter or any of the direction keys.

Remember: In Excel, a cell can hold as many as 32,767 characters.

If you enter text that's longer than its column's current width, one of two things happens:

✦ If the cells to the immediate right are blank, Excel displays the text in its entirety, spilling the entry into adjacent cells.

✦ If an adjacent cell is not blank, Excel displays as much of the text as possible. (The full text is contained in the cell; it's just not displayed.)

In either case, you can always see the text that you're typing because it appears in the formula bar as well as in the cell.

Remember: If you need to display a long text entry that's adjacent to a cell with an entry, you can edit your text to make it shorter, increase the width of the column, or wrap the text within the cell so that it occupies more than one line.

If you have lengthy text in a cell, you can force Excel to display it in multiple lines within the cell. Use Alt+Enter to start a new line in a cell. When you add this line break, Excel automatically changes the cell's format to Wrap Text.

See also "Wrapping text within a cell," in Part III.

Entering the same data into a range of cells

If you need to enter the same data (value, text, or formula) into multiple cells, your first inclination may be to enter it once and then copy it to the remaining cells. Here's a better way:

1. Select all the cells that you want to contain the data.

2. Enter the value, text, or formula into one cell.

3. Press Ctrl+Enter.

The single entry is inserted into each cell in the selection.

Entering values into cells

To enter a numeric value into a cell, follow these steps:

1. Move the cell pointer to the appropriate cell.

2. Enter the value.

3. Press Enter or any of the direction keys.

The value displays in the cell, and it also appears in the Excel formula bar. You can also include a decimal point, dollar sign, plus sign, minus sign, and comma. If you precede a value with a minus sign or enclose it in parentheses, Excel considers the value to be a negative number.

Remember: Sometimes the value isn't displayed exactly as you enter it. Excel may convert very large numbers to scientific notation. The formula bar always displays the value that you originally enter.

Erasing Data in Cells and Ranges

To erase the contents of a cell but leave the cell's formatting and cell comments intact, perform the following two steps:

1. Select the cell or range you want to erase.

2. Press Delete.

For more control over what gets deleted, you can use the Edit➪ Clear command. This menu item leads to a submenu with four additional choices.

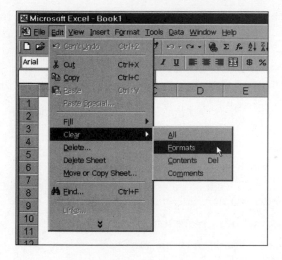

All: Clears everything from the cell.

Formats: Clears only the formatting and leaves the value, text, or formula.

Contents: Clears only the cell's contents and leaves the formatting.

Comments: Clears the comment (if one exists) attached to the cell.

Moving Cells and Ranges

Moving the data in a cell or a range is common. For example, you may need to relocate a range of data to make room for something else.

Moving by dragging

Here's how to move a cell or range by dragging it:

1. Select the cell or range that you want to move.

2. Move the mouse pointer to one of the four borders of the selected cell or range.

   When you do so, the mouse pointer turns into an arrow.

3. Drag the selection to its new location and release the mouse button.

This is similar to copying a cell, except that you don't press Ctrl while dragging.

Remember: If the mouse pointer does not turn into an arrow in Step 2, it means that the drag and drop feature is turned off. To turn the feature on, follow these steps:

1. Select the Tools⇨Options command.

2. Click the Edit tab.

3. Check the check box labeled Allow cell drag and drop.

Moving data to a different worksheet or workbook

If you want to move the contents of a cell or range to a different worksheet or to a different workbook, follow these steps:

1. Select the cell or range to move.

2. Select the Edit⇨Cut command.

Or you can press Ctrl+X or click the Cut button on the Standard toolbar.

3. Activate the worksheet that you're moving to. If you're moving the selection to a different workbook, activate that workbook and then activate the worksheet.

4. Move the cell pointer to the range that you want to hold the copy (you need only select the upper-left cell).

5. Press Enter.

When you move data, make sure that there are enough blank cells to hold it. Excel overwrites existing data without warning.

Remember: If you change your mind after Step 2, press Esc to cancel the operation. If you change your mind after the data has already been moved, choose the Edit⇨Undo Paste command or press Ctrl+Z.

Moving data to a new location in the same worksheet

Here's how to move a cell or range:

1. Select the cell or range to move.

2. Select the Edit⇨Cut command.

Or you can press Ctrl+X or click the Cut button on the Standard toolbar.

3. Move the cell pointer to the range that you want to hold the copy (you need only select the upper-left cell).

4. Press Enter.

If the range that you're moving contains formulas that refer to other cells, the references continue to refer to the original cells. You almost always want references to continue to refer to the original cells.

When you move data, make sure that there are enough blank cells to hold it. Excel overwrites existing data without warning.

Remember: If you change your mind after Step 2, press Esc to cancel the operation. If you change your mind after you've already moved the data, choose Edit⇨Undo Paste or press Ctrl+Z.

Replacing the Contents of a Cell

To replace the contents of a cell with something else, follow these steps:

1. Select the cell.

2. Make your new entry (it replaces the previous contents).

Any formatting that you applied to the cell remains.

Searching for Data

If your worksheet contains lots of data, you may find it difficult to locate a particular piece of information. A quick way to do so is to let Excel do it for you.

To locate a particular value or sequence of text, follow these steps:

1. Select the area of the worksheet that you want to search. If you want to search the entire worksheet, just select a single cell (any cell will do).

2. Choose the Edit⇨Find command or press Ctrl+F.

Excel displays its Find dialog box.

3. In the Find what box, enter the characters to search for. (If you want to make your search case sensitive, put a check mark in the Match case check box.)

4. In the Look in box, specify what to look in: Formulas, Values, or Comments.

5. Click the Find Next button.

Excel selects the cell that contains what you're looking for.

6. If there is more than one occurrence, repeat Step 5 until you find the cell that you're looking for.

7. Click the Close button to end.

For approximate searches, use *wildcard characters*. An asterisk represents any group of characters in the specified position, and a question mark represents any single character in the specified position. For example, **w*h** represents all text that begins with *w* and ends with *h*. Similarly, **b?n** matches three-letter words such as bin, bun, and ban.

See also "Searching and Replacing Data," in this part.

Searching and Replacing Data

Sometimes you may need to replace all occurrences of a value or text with something else. Excel makes this easy to do:

1. Select the area of the worksheet that you want to search. If you want to search the entire worksheet, just select a single cell (any cell will do).

2. Choose the Edit➪Replace command or press Ctrl+H.

Excel displays the Replace dialog box.

3. In the Find what box enter the characters to search for.

4. In the Replace with box, enter the characters to replace them.

5. Click the Replace All button to have Excel search and replace automatically.

If you want to verify each replacement, click the Find Next button. Excel pauses when it finds a match. To replace the found text, click Replace. To skip it and find the next match, click the Find Next button again.

6. Click the Close button when you are finished.

See also "Searching for Data," in this part.

Selecting Cells and Ranges

In Excel, you normally select a cell or range before performing an operation that works with the cell or range. Topics in this section describe how to make various types of cell and range selections.

Selecting a cell

To select a cell (and make it the active cell), use any of the following techniques:

✦ Move the cell pointer to the cell using the arrow keys.

✦ Click the cell with the mouse.

✦ Use the Edit⇨Go To command (or press F5 or Ctrl+G), enter the cell address in the Reference box, and click OK.

The selected cell has a dark border around it, and its address appears in the Name box.

Selecting entire rows and columns

You can select entire rows or columns in several ways:

✦ Click the row or column heading to select a single row or column.

✦ To select multiple adjacent rows or columns, simply click a row or column heading and drag to highlight additional rows or columns.

✦ To select multiple (nonadjacent) rows or columns, press Ctrl while you click the row or column headings that you want.

✦ Press Ctrl+spacebar to select the column of the active cell or the columns of the selected cells.

✦ Press Shift+spacebar to select the row of the active cell or the rows of the selected cells.

✦ Click the Select All button (or Ctrl+Shift+spacebar) to select all rows. Selecting all rows is the same as selecting all columns, which is the same as selecting all cells.

Selecting a multisheet (3-D) range

An Excel workbook can contain more than one worksheet, and a range can extend across multiple worksheets. You can think of these as three-dimensional ranges.

To select a multisheet range, follow these steps:

1. Select the range on the active sheet.

2. Press Ctrl and click the sheet tabs of the other sheets to include in the selection.

Notice that the workbook's title bar displays [Group]. This is a reminder that you've selected a group of sheets and that you're in

Group Edit mode. The range that you selected will also be selected on each sheet in the group.

After you select a multisheet range, you can perform the same operations that you can perform on a single sheet range.

If the multisheet range consists of a contiguous worksheet, you can press Shift and then click the tab of the last sheet to be included. Pressing Shift selects all sheets from the active sheet up to and including the sheet that you click.

Selecting noncontiguous ranges

Most of the time, the ranges that you select will be *contiguous* — a single rectangle of cells. Excel also lets you work with noncontiguous ranges, which consist of two or more ranges (or single cells), not necessarily next to each other (also known as a *multiple selection*).

If you want to apply the same formatting to cells in different areas of your worksheet, one approach is to make a multiple selection. After you select the appropriate cells or ranges, Excel applies the formatting that you choose to all the selected cells.

	A	B	C	D	E	F	G
1							
2	Apples	10	9	9	7	8	
3	Oranges	32	36	40	42	46	
4	Pears	72	75	76	82	87	
5	Bananas	50	60	67	73	77	
6							
7							
8							
9							
10							
11							

Bill.xls — Sheet1

You can select a noncontiguous range in several ways:

✦ Hold down Ctrl while you click the mouse and drag to highlight the individual cells or ranges.

✦ From the keyboard, select a range by pressing F8 and then use the arrow keys. After selecting the first range, press Shift+F8, move the cell pointer, and press F8 to start selecting another range.

✦ Use the Edit⇨Go To command (or press F5 or Ctrl+G) and enter a range's address in the Reference box. Separate the different ranges with a comma. Click OK, and Excel selects the cells in the ranges that you specified.

Selecting a range

You can select a range in several ways:

✦ Click the mouse in a cell and drag to highlight the range. If you drag to the end of the screen, the worksheet scrolls.

✦ Move to the first cell of the range. Press F8 and then move the cell pointer with the direction keys to highlight the range. Press F8 again to return the direction keys to normal movement.

✦ Press the Shift key while you use the arrow keys to select a range.

✦ Use the Edit⇨Go To command (or press F5), enter a range's address in the Reference box, and click OK.

When you select a range in Excel 2000, Excel shows the range in the See-Through View. Instead of appearing in reversed video like older versions of Excel, the cells appear as if behind a transparent colored shade. This transparent selection makes it easier to see the true colors and formatting underneath the selection.

Special selections

Excel provides a way to select only "special" cells in the workbook or in a selected range. These are cells that contain a certain type of information (see the table that follows).

1. Choose the Edit⇨Go To command, which brings up the Go To dialog box. (You can also press F5 or Ctrl+G.)

2. Click the Special button, displaying the Go To Special dialog box.

The following text describes some of the options available in this dialog box.

• **Comments:** Selects only the cells that contain cell comments (*see* "Using Cell Comments," in this part).

• **Constants:** Selects all nonempty cells that don't contain formulas. This is useful if you have a model set up, and you want to clear out all input cells and enter new values. The formulas remain intact.

• **Formulas:** Selects cells that contain formulas. You can further qualify this by selecting the type of result: Numbers, Text, Logicals (true or false), or Errors.

• **Blanks:** Selects all empty cells.

• **Current region:** Selects a rectangular range of cells around the active cell. This range is determined by surrounding blank rows and columns. Ctrl+Shift+* is the shortcut key for this option.

- **Current array:** Selects the entire array. An *array* is a special type of formula used by advanced users.

- **Objects:** Selects all graphic objects on the worksheet.

- **Row differences:** Analyzes the selection and selects cells that are different from other cells in each row. Ctrl +\ is the shortcut for row differences.

- **Column differences:** Analyzes the selection and selects the cells that are different from other cells in each column. Ctrl +Shift+ | is the shortcut for this option.

- **Precedents:** Selects cells that are referred to in the formulas in the active cell or the selection. You can select either direct precedents or precedents at all levels (these options appear below the Dependents option).

- **Dependents:** Selects cells with formulas that refer to the active cell or the selection. You can select either direct dependents or dependents at all levels.

- **Last cell:** Selects the bottom-right cell in the worksheet that contains data or formatting. Ctrl+End is the shortcut for this option.

- **Visible cells only:** Selects only visible cells in the selection. This feature is useful when dealing with outlines or an AutoFiltered list (*see* Part VI).

- **Conditional formats:** Selects cells that have conditional formats.

- **Data validation:** Selects cells that are validated when data is entered.

  After making your choice in the dialog box, Excel selects the qualifying subset of cells in the current selection. Usually, this results in a multiple selection (that is, a selection of noncontiguous cells).

Remember: If you bring up the Go To Special dialog box with only one cell selected, Excel bases its selection on the active area of the worksheet. If no cells qualify, Excel lets you know.

Transposing a range

If you need to change the orientation of a range, Excel can do it for you in a snap. When you transpose a range, rows become columns and columns become rows.

The following figure shows an example of a horizontal range that was transposed to a vertical range.

Horizontal range   Vertical range

monthly.xls							
	A	B	C	D	E	F	G
1							
2	Jan	Feb	Mar	Apr	May	Jun	
3	450	489	522	512	566	602	
4							
5							
6		Jan	450				
7		Feb	489				
8		Mar	522				
9		Apr	512				
10		May	566				
11		Jun	602				
12							
13							

Sheet1

To transpose a range, do the following:

1. Select the range to transpose.

2. Choose the Edit⇨Copy command (or press Ctrl+C or click the Copy button on the Standard toolbar).

3. Activate the upper-left cell where you want the transposed range to be.

The transposed range cannot overlap with the original range.

4. Choose the Edit⇨Paste Special command.

5. Check the Transpose check box in the Paste Special dialog box.

6. Click OK.

7. Delete the original range, if necessary.

Remember: Excel adjusts any formulas in the original range so they work properly when transposed.

Undoing Changes and Mistakes

One very useful feature in Excel is its multilevel undo. This means that you can reverse your recent actions, one step at a time. For example, if you discover that you accidentally deleted a range of data several minutes ago, you can use the undo feature to "backtrack" through your actions until the deleted range reappears.

Remember: Undoing your actions can only be done in a sequential manner. In other words, if you want to undo an action you must also undo all of the actions that you performed after the action that you want to undo. You can undo the past 16 operations that you performed.

To undo an operation, use any of the following techniques:

✦ Select the Edit⇨Undo command. The command tells you what you will be undoing.

✦ Press Ctrl+Z or Ctrl+Backspace until you arrive at the action that you want to undo.

✦ Click the Undo button on the Standard toolbar until you arrive at the action that you want to undo.

✦ Click the arrow on the Undo button on the Standard toolbar. This displays a description of your recent actions. Select the actions to undo.

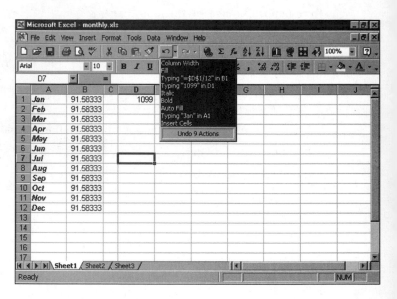

Using AutoComplete

AutoComplete enables you to type the first few letters of a text entry into a cell, and Excel automatically completes the entry based on other entries that you've already made in the column.

AutoComplete works with no effort on your part:

1. Begin entering text or a value.

2. If Excel recognizes your entry, it automatically completes it.

3. If Excel guesses correctly, press Enter to accept it. If you want to enter something else, just continue typing and ignore Excel's guess.

You also can access this feature by right-clicking the cell and selecting Pic<u>k</u> from list. With this method, Excel displays a drop-down list with all of the entries in the current column. Just click the one that you want, and it's entered automatically.

If you don't like this feature, you can turn it off in the Edit panel of the Options dialog box. Remove the check mark from the check box labeled Enable Auto<u>C</u>omplete for Cell Values.

Using AutoFill

AutoFill is a handy feature that has several uses (mouse required). AutoFill uses the fill handle — the small square that appears at the bottom-right corner of the selected cell or range.

If you right-click and drag a fill handle, Excel displays a shortcut menu of fill options.

Fill handle

monthly.xls						
	A	B	C	D	E	F	G

Cell A2: 9/1/98

Cell C3: 9/3/98

Shortcut menu:
- <u>C</u>opy Cells
- Fill <u>S</u>eries
- Fill <u>F</u>ormats
- Fill <u>V</u>alues
- Fill <u>D</u>ays
- Fill <u>W</u>eekdays
- Fill <u>M</u>onths
- Fill <u>Y</u>ears
- Linear Trend
- Growth Trend
- Series...

Sheet3 / Sheet2 / Sheet1

Remember: If the selected cell or range does not have a fill handle, it means that this feature is turned off. To turn AutoFill on, follow these steps:

1. Select the Tools⇨Options command.

2. Click the Edit tab.

3. Check the check box labeled Allow cell drag and drop.

You cannot use AutoFill when you've made a multiple selection.

For more on AutoFill, *see Excel 2000 For Windows For Dummies,* by Greg Harvey (from IDG Books Worldwide, Inc.).

Entering a series of incremental values or dates

To use AutoFill to enter a series of incremental values, follow these steps:

1. Enter at least two values or dates in the series into adjacent cells. These values need not be consecutive.

2. Select the cells you used in Step 1.

3. Click and drag the fill handle to complete the series in the cells that you select.

While you drag the fill handle, Excel displays a small box that tells you what it's planning to enter into each cell.

Remember: If you drag the fill handle when only one cell is selected, Excel examines the data and determines whether to increment the value or simply copy it. For more control, drag the fill handle while pressing the right mouse button. When you release the button, you get a list of options.

AutoFill also works in the negative direction. For example, if you use AutoFill by starting with two cells that contain **–20** and **–19,** Excel fills in –18, –17, and so on.

If the values in the cells that you enter do not have equal increments, Excel completes the series by calculating a simple linear regression. This feature is handy for performing simple forecasts. *Note:* Excel calculates a simple linear regression or progression, depending on the direction (negative or positive) of the series.

Entering a series of text

Excel is familiar with some text series (days of the week, month names), and it can complete these series for you automatically.

Here's how to use AutoFill to complete a known series of text:

1. Enter any of the series into a cell (for example, **Monday** or **February**).

2. Click and drag the fill handle to complete the series in the cells that you select.

You can also teach Excel to recognize custom lists. Choose Tools➪ Options and click the Custom Lists tab. Click the NEW LIST option and enter your list in the box labeled List entries. Click Add to store the list. Your custom list also works with AutoFill.

Using Automatic Decimal Points

If you're entering lots of numbers with a fixed number of decimal places, you can save some time by letting Excel enter the decimal point (like the feature available on some adding machines).

1. Select the Tools➪Options command.

2. Click the Edit tab.

3. Check the check box labeled Fixed decimal and make sure that it's set for the number of decimal places that you want to use.

Excel now supplies the decimal points for you automatically. For example, if you have it set for two decimal places and you enter **12345** into a cell, Excel interprets it as 123.45 (it adds the decimal point). To restore things to normal, just uncheck the Fixed Decimal check box in the Options dialog box.

Remember: Changing this setting doesn't affect any values that you have already entered.

Using Cell Comments

The Excel cell comment feature enables you to attach a comment to a cell — useful when you need to document a particular value or to help you remember what a formula does. When you move the mouse pointer over a cell that has a comment, the comment pops up in a small box.

Adding a cell comment

To add a comment to a cell, follow these steps:

1. Select the cell.

2. Choose the Insert➪Comment command (or press Shift+F2).

Excel displays a text box that points to the cell.

3. Enter the text for the comment into the text box.

4. Click any cell when you're finished.

	A	B	C	D	E	F	
1							
2	Growth Factor	0.75%	**Rob Wallace:**				
3			This number must be				
4	January	1,044.00	approved by Jill before				
5	February	1,051.83	this is submitted.				
6	March	1,059.72					
7	April	1,067.67					
8	May	1,075.67					
9	June	1,083.74					
10	July	1,091.87					
11	August	1,100.06					
12	September	1,108.31					
13	October	1,116.62					
14	November	1,125.00					
15	December	1,133.43					
16							

monthly.xls — Sheet4 / Employees / Sheet2 / She

The cell displays a small red triangle to indicate that the cell contains a comment.

Editing a cell comment

To edit a cell comment, select the cell that contains the comment and then choose the Insert⇨Edit Comment command. Or you can right-click and choose Edit Comment from the shortcut menu.

Viewing cell comments

Cells that have a comment attached display a small red triangle in the upper-right corner. When you move the mouse pointer over a cell that contains a comment, Excel displays the comment.

To view the comments in all cells, choose the View⇨Comments command.

Using Data Entry Forms

If you're entering data that is arranged in rows, you may find it helpful to use Excel's built-in data form for data entry.

Using Excel's built-in data form

To enter data using a data entry form, follow these steps:

1. If your data entry range does not have descriptive headings in the first row, enter some headings. You can always erase these headings later if you don't need them.

2. Select any cell in the header row.

3. Choose the <u>D</u>ata⇔<u>F</u>orm command.

Excel asks whether you want to use that row for headers (click OK). It then displays a dialog box with edit boxes and several buttons.

4. Enter data into the edit boxes, using Tab to move between the boxes. When you complete entering the data for a row, click the Ne<u>w</u> button. Click C<u>l</u>ose when finished.

Excel dumps the data into the worksheet and clears the dialog box for the next row.

See also "Filtering and Sorting Lists," in Part VI.

Part V

Using Formulas and Functions

This part deals with topics related to formulas and functions. It also covers related topics that deal with data consolidation and auditing.

In this part . . .

✔ **Consolidating data in multiple worksheets**

✔ **Entering formulas**

✔ **Working with formulas that contain links**

✔ **Creating and using range names**

✔ **Using the built-in worksheet functions in Excel**

✔ **Identifying worksheet errors**

Consolidating Data

Data consolidation refers to the process of merging data from multiple worksheets or multiple workbook files. For example, a division manager may consolidate various departmental budgets into a single workbook.

The main factor that determines how easy a consolidation task will be is whether the information is laid out exactly the same way in each worksheet. If so, the job is relatively simple.

If the worksheets have little or no resemblance to each other, your best bet may be to edit each sheet so they match each other. In some cases, it may be more efficient to simply reenter the information in a standard format.

Any of the following techniques consolidate information from multiple worksheets or workbooks:

✦ Use formulas (link formulas if the data is in multiple workbooks).

✦ Use the Data➪Consolidate command.

✦ Use a pivot table.

See also "Pivot Tables," in Part VI.

Consolidating data by matching labels

If the worksheets you want to consolidate are not laid out identically, you may still be able to use Excel's Data➪Consolidate command. The worksheets must have identical row and column labels, because Excel uses this information to match the data. Here's how:

1. Start with a new workbook.

The source workbooks can be open, but this is not necessary.

2. Select the Data➪Consolidate command to open the Consolidate dialog box.

3. Select the type of consolidation summary that you want.

Most of the time you'll use Sum, which adds the corresponding values together.

4. Enter the range reference for the first worksheet.

If the workbook is open, you can point to the reference. If it's not open, click the Browse button to locate the file on disk. The reference must include a range. When the reference in the Reference box is correct, click Add to add it to the All references list.

5. Repeat Step 4 for each additional worksheet that you want to consolidate.

6. Because the worksheets aren't laid out the same, select the Left Column and Top Row check boxes to match the data by using the labels in the worksheet.

7. Click OK to begin the consolidation.

See also "Using the Consolidate dialog box," in this part, for an explanation of the various options in the Consolidate dialog box.

Consolidating data by position

If the worksheets you want to consolidate are laid out identically, your job is much easier because Excel doesn't have to match labels to identify the data (see "Consolidating data by matching labels," in this part). Here's how:

1. Start with a new workbook.

The source workbooks can be open, but this is not necessary.

2. Select the Data⇨Consolidate command to display the Consolidate dialog box.

3. Select the type of consolidation summary that you want.

Most of the time you'll use Sum, which adds the corresponding values together.

4. Enter the range reference for the first worksheet.

If the workbook is open, you can point to the reference. If it's not open, click the Browse button to locate the file on disk. The reference must include a range. When the reference in the Reference box is correct, click Add to add it to the All references list.

5. Repeat Step 4 for each additional worksheet that you want to consolidate.

6. Click OK to begin the consolidation.

Excel creates the consolidation beginning at the active cell.

See also "Using the Consolidate dialog box," in this part, for an explanation of the various options in the Consolidate dialog box.

Consolidating data by using formulas

You can consolidate information across worksheets by creating formulas that refer to cells in the source worksheets. To consolidate data by using formulas, do the following:

1. Start with an empty worksheet.

2. Enter a formula that uses the cells in each of the source worksheets (this task is much easier if all of the workbooks are open).

3. If the source worksheets are laid out identically, copy the formula created in Step 2.

If the source worksheets have different layouts, you need to create each formula separately.

Remember: Using formulas in this manner ensures that the consolidation formulas are updated if the source data changes.

See also "Referencing cells in other workbooks" and "Referencing cells in other worksheets," both in this part.

Using the Consolidate dialog box

Following are descriptions of the options in the Consolidate dialog box:

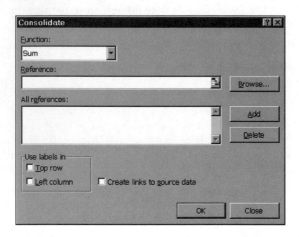

Function: This is where you specify the type of consolidation. Most of the time you use Sum, but you also can select from ten other options.

Reference: This holds a range from a source file that will be consolidated. After you enter the range, click the Add button to add it to the All references list. If you're consolidating by position, don't include labels in the range. If you're consolidating by matching labels, *do* include labels in the range.

All references: This list box contains the list of references that you have added with the Add button.

Use labels in: These check boxes tell Excel to examine the labels in the Top row, the Left column, or both positions to perform the consolidation. Use these options when you're consolidating by category.

Create links to source data: This option, when selected, creates an outline in the destination worksheet that consists of external references to the destination cells (that is, link formulas). In addition, the outline includes summary formulas. If this option isn't selected, the consolidation doesn't use formulas. If you create links, it is easier to update the destination worksheet if data in any of the source worksheets changes.

Browse: This button displays a dialog box that lets you select a workbook on disk. It inserts the filename in the Reference box, but you have to supply the range reference.

Add: This button adds the reference in the Reference box to the All references list.

Delete: This button deletes the selected reference from the All references list.

See also "Consolidating data by position" and "Consolidating data by matching labels," both in this part.

Using Formulas

A formula can consist of up to 1,024 characters and any of the following elements:

✦ Operators such as + (for addition) and * (for multiplication)

✦ Cell references (including named cells and ranges)

✦ Values, text, or logical values

✦ Worksheet functions (such as SUM or AVERAGE)

When you enter a formula into a cell, the cell displays the result of the formula. You see the formula itself in the formula bar when the cell is activated.

The following table provides the list of operators that you can use in formulas.

Operator	Name
+	Addition
−	Subtraction
*	Multiplication
/	Division
^	Exponentiation (raised to a power)
&	Concatenation (joins text)
=	Logical comparison (equal to)
>	Logical comparison (greater than)
<	Logical comparison (less than)

Operator precedence is the set of rules that Excel uses to perform its calculations in a formula. The following table lists the Excel operator precedence. This table shows that exponentiation has the highest precedence (that is, it's performed first), and logical comparisons have the lowest precedence. If two operators have the same precedence, Excel performs the calculations from left to right.

Remember: You can override operator precedence by using parentheses in your formulas.

Symbol	Operator	Precedence
^	Exponentiation	1
*	Multiplication	2
/	Division	2
+	Addition	3
−	Subtraction	3
&	Concatenation	4
=	Equal to	5
>	Greater than	5
<	Less than	5

For more on using formulas, see *Excel 2000 For Windows For Dummies* by Greg Harvey (from IDG Books Worldwide, Inc.).

Calculating subtotals

The ability that Excel has to create subtotal formulas automatically is handy and can save you lots of time. To use this feature, you must have a list that is sorted.

To insert subtotal formulas into a list, follow these steps:

1. Move the cell pointer anywhere in the list.

2. Choose <u>D</u>ata⇨Su<u>b</u>totals.

3. Complete the Subtotal dialog box by specifying the options described in the following text.

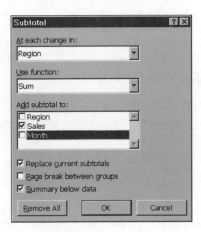

The formulas all use the Subtotal worksheet function to insert the subtotals.

- **<u>A</u>t each change in:** This drop-down list displays the columns in your list. The column that you choose must be sorted.

- **<u>U</u>se function:** This box gives you a choice of 11 functions. Usually, you'll want to use Sum (the default).

- **A<u>d</u>d subtotal to:** This list box lists all of the fields in your list. Place a check mark next to the field or fields that you want to subtotal.

- **Replace <u>c</u>urrent subtotals:** If this box is checked, any existing subtotal formulas are removed and replaced with the new subtotals.

- **<u>P</u>age break between groups:** If this box is checked, Excel inserts a manual page break after each subtotal.

- **<u>S</u>ummary below data:** If this box is checked, the subtotals are placed below the data (the default). Otherwise, the subtotal formulas are placed above the totals.

- **<u>R</u>emove All:** This button removes all of the subtotal formulas in the list.

4. Click OK and Excel analyzes the list and inserts formulas as specified — and also creates an outline for you.

See also "Outlining Your Worksheet," in Part III.

Changing the source of links

If your workbook uses one or more formulas that contain links to other workbooks, you may need to change the source workbook for your external references. For example, you may have a worksheet that has links to a workbook named Preliminary Budget. Later, you get a finalized version named Final Budget.

To change the link source, follow these steps:

1. Select the Edit⇨Links command.

2. In the Links dialog box, select the source workbook that you want to change.

3. Click the Change Source button.

4. In the Change Links dialog box, select a new source file and then click OK.

After you select the file, all external reference formulas are updated.

Changing when formulas are calculated

When the Excel Calculation mode is set to Automatic (the default setting), changing cells that are used in a formula causes the formula to display a new result automatically. Excel follows these rules when calculating your worksheet:

✦ When you make a change (enter or edit data or formulas, for example), Excel immediately recalculates those formulas that depend on new or edited data.

✦ If Excel is in the middle of a lengthy calculation, the calculation is temporarily suspended while you perform other worksheet tasks; it resumes when you're finished.

✦ Formulas are evaluated in a natural sequence. In other words, if a formula in cell D12 depends on the result of a formula in cell D11, cell D11 is calculated before D12.

To set the Excel Calculation mode to Manual, follow these steps:

1. Choose the Tools⇨Options command.

2. Click the Calculation tab.

3. Click the Manual option button.

When you switch to Manual Calculation mode, the Recalculate before save check box is automatically turned on. You can turn this off if you want to speed up file-save operations.

Remember: When you're working in Manual Calculation mode, Excel displays Calculate in the status bar when you have any uncalculated formulas. Use the following shortcut keys to recalculate the formulas:

✦ F9: Calculates the formulas in all open workbooks.

✦ Shift+F9: Calculates only the formulas in the active worksheet. Other worksheets in the same workbook aren't calculated.

Remember: The Excel Calculation mode isn't specific to a particular worksheet. When you change the Calculation mode, all open workbooks are affected, not just the active workbook.

Converting formulas to values

Sometimes, you may want to convert a formula to its current value (remove the formula and leave only its result). To do so, follow these steps:

1. Select the cell that contains the formula. If you want to convert several formulas you can select a range.

 2. Choose the Edit⇨Copy command (you can also press Ctrl+C or click the Copy button on the Standard toolbar).

3. Choose the Edit⇨Paste Special command.

4. In the Paste Special dialog box, select the Values option button.

5. Click OK.

6. Press Enter to cancel Copy mode.

Remember: The preceding procedure overwrites the formulas. If you want to put the current values of the formulas in a different (empty) area of the worksheet, select a different range before Step 3 in the preceding list.

Identifying formula errors

Excel flags errors in formulas with a message that begins with a pound sign (#). This signals that the formula is returning an error value. You have to correct the formula (or correct a cell that is referenced by the formula) to get rid of the error display.

Remember: If the entire cell is filled with pound signs, the column isn't wide enough to display the value.

The following table lists the types of error values that may appear in a cell that has a formula.

Error Value	Explanation
#DIV/0!	The formula is trying to divide by zero (an operation that's not allowed on this planet). This also occurs when the formula attempts to divide by an empty cell.
#NAME?	The formula uses a name that Excel doesn't recognize. This can happen if you delete a name that's used in the formula or if you have unmatched quotes when using text.
#N/A	The formula is referring (directly or indirectly) to a cell that uses the NA functions to signal the fact that data is not available.
#NULL!	The formula uses an intersection of two ranges that don't intersect.
#NUM!	There is a problem with a value; for example, you specified a negative number where a positive number is expected.
#REF!	The formula refers to a cell that isn't valid. This can happen if the cell has been deleted from the worksheet.
#VALUE!	The formula has a function with an invalid argument, or the formula uses an operand of the wrong type (such as text where a value is expected).

Remember: A single error value can make its way to lots of other cells that contain formulas that depend on the cell.

Pasting names into a formula

If your formula uses named cells or ranges, you can type the name in place of the address. A less error-prone approach is to choose the name from a list and have Excel insert the name for you automatically. You can do this in two ways:

✦ Select the Insert⇨Name⇨Paste command. Excel displays its Paste Name dialog box with all of the names listed. Select the name and click OK.

✦ Press F3. This command also displays the Paste Name dialog box.

See also topics in "Using Names," in this part.

Referencing cells in other workbooks

If your formula needs to refer to a cell in a different workbook, use this format for your formula:

```
=[WorkbookName]SheetName!CellAddress
```

The workbook name (in brackets), the worksheet name, and an exclamation point precede the cell address. Such a formula is sometimes known as a *link formula* or an *external reference.*

Remember: If the workbook name in the reference includes one or more spaces, you must enclose it (and the sheet name) in single quotation marks. For example, here's a formula that refers to a cell on Sheet1 in a workbook named Budget For 1999:

```
=A1*'[Budget For 1999]Sheet1'!A1
```

When a formula refers to cells in a different workbook, the other workbook doesn't need to be open. If the workbook is closed, you must add the complete path to the reference. Here's an example:

```
=A1*'C:\MSOffice\Excel\[Budget For 1999]Sheet1'!A1
```

Referencing cells in other worksheets

If your formula needs to refer to a cell in a different worksheet in the same workbook, use the following format for your formula:

```
SheetName!CellAddress
```

Precede the cell address with the worksheet name, followed by an exclamation point.

Remember: If the worksheet name in the reference includes one or more spaces, you must enclose it in single quotation marks. Here's a formula that refers to a cell on a sheet named All Depts:

```
=A1*'All Depts'!A1
```

Severing (cutting) links

If you have external references in a workbook (that is, a link to a different workbook) and then decide that you don't want them, you can convert the external reference formulas to values, thereby severing the links:

1. Select the cell or range that contains the external reference formulas.

2. Click the Copy button on the Standard toolbar to copy the selection to the Clipboard.

You can also press Ctrl+C to copy the selection to the clipboard.

3. Choose the Edit⇨Paste Special command.

4. In the Paste Special dialog box, select the Values option.

5. Click OK.

6. Press Enter to cancel Copy mode.

All formulas in the selected range are converted to their current values.

Updating links

To ensure that your link formulas have the latest values from their source workbooks, you can force an update. Forcing an update may be necessary if you've just learned that an updated version of a source workbook has been saved to your network server.

To update linked formulas with their current value, follow these steps:

1. Select the Edit⇨Links command.

2. In the Links dialog box, choose the appropriate source workbook.

3. Click the Update Now button.

Excel updates the link formulas.

Using absolute, relative, and mixed references

An *absolute reference* uses two dollar signs in its address: one for the column part and one for the row part. When you copy a formula that has an absolute reference, the reference is not adjusted in the copied cell. *Relative references,* on the other hand, are adjusted when the formula is copied.

Excel also allows mixed references in which only one of the address's parts is absolute. The following table summarizes all of the possible types of cell references.

Example	Type
A1	Relative reference
A1	Absolute reference
$A1	Mixed reference (column part is absolute)
A$1	Mixed reference (row part is absolute)

To change the type of cell reference in a formula, follow these steps:

1. Double-click the cell (or press F2) to get into edit mode.

2. In the formula bar, move the cursor to a cell reference.

3. Press F4 repeatedly to cycle through all possible cell reference types. Stop when the cell reference displays the proper type.

Using the Formula Palette

If you need assistance entering or editing formulas, you can use the Formula Palette. To access the Formula Palette, click the Edit Formula button (=) in the formula bar.

✦ If the active cell is empty, you can enter a formula into the cell.

✦ If the active cell already contains a formula, you can use the Formula Palette to edit the formula.

The Formula Palette displays the result of the formula as it is being entered. If you need to use a function in your formula, select it from the function list (which occupies the space normally used by the Name box on the left side of the formula bar).

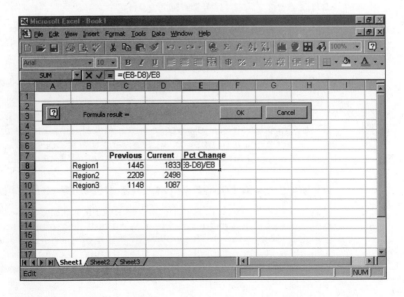

See also "Using the Formula Palette to enter functions," in this part.

Using Functions in Your Formulas

Excel provides more than 300 built-in functions that can make your formulas perform powerful feats and save you a great deal of time.

Functions do the following:

✦ Simplify your formulas

✦ Allow formulas to perform calculations that are otherwise impossible

✦ Allow "conditional" execution of formulas — giving them some rudimentary decision-making capability

You can use the Excel VBA language to create your own custom functions if you're so inclined.

Most, but not all, worksheet functions use one or more arguments, enclosed in parentheses. Think of an argument as a piece of information that clarifies what you want the function to do. For example, the following function (which rounds the number in cell A1 to two decimal places) uses two arguments:

=ROUND(A1,2)

Entering functions manually

If you're familiar with the function that you want to use, you may choose to simply type the function and its arguments into your formula. Often this is the most efficient method.

Remember: If you're using a function at the beginning of a formula, you must provide an initial equal sign (=).

When you enter a function, Excel always converts it to uppercase. It's a good idea to use lowercase when entering functions: If Excel doesn't convert it to uppercase, it means that it doesn't recognize your entry as a function (you probably spelled it incorrectly).

Modifying a range reference used in a function

When you edit a cell that contains a formula, Excel color-codes the references in the formula and places an outline around each cell or range referenced in the formula. The color of the outline corresponds to the color displayed in the formula. Each outlined cell or range also contains a fill handle (a small square in the lower-left corner).

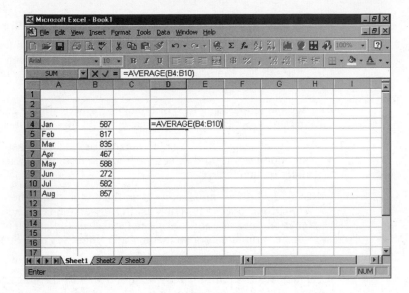

If your formula contains a function that uses a range argument, you can easily modify the range reference by following these steps:

1. To begin editing the formula, press F2, double-click the cell, or click the Edit Formula icon (=) in the formula bar.

2. Locate the range that the function uses (the range is outlined).

3. Drag the fill handle to extend or contract the range. Or, you can click a border of the outlined range and move the outline to a new range. In either case, Excel changes the range reference in the formula.

4. Press Enter.

Using add-in functions

Some functions are available only when a particular add-in is open. To use add-in worksheet functions, follow these steps:

1. Select the Tools⇨Add-Ins command.

2. Check the box next to the add-in that contains the functions you need.

3. Click OK.

You can then use the add-in functions in your formulas.

Remember: If you attempt to use an add-in function when the add-in is not loaded, the formula will display #NAME?

Using the Formula Palette to enter functions

The Formula Palette makes it easy to enter a function and its arguments. Using this tool ensures that the function is spelled correctly and has the proper number of arguments in the correct order.

To enter a function using the Formula Palette, activate the cell that will contain the function and then use either of these two methods:

✦ Select the Insert⇨Function command (or click the Paste Function button) and select the function from the Paste Function dialog box.

✦ Click the Edit Formula icon (=) on the edit line and then select a function from the function list in the Name box. If the function does not appear on the list, select the More Functions option and choose the function from the Paste Function dialog box.

Excel displays the Formula Palette directly below the edit line (you can drag it to a new location if it's in your way). The Formula Palette prompts you for each argument of the function you selected. You can enter the arguments manually or (if they are cell references) point to them in the worksheet. The Formula Palette displays the result. When you've specified all of the required arguments, click OK.

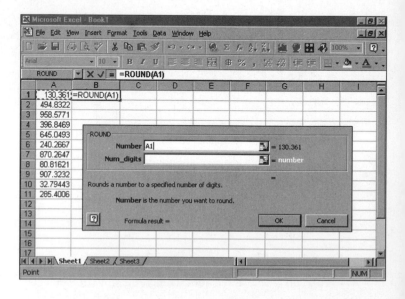

✦ You can use the Formula Palette to insert a function into an existing formula. Click the Edit Formula button (=) to bring up the Formula Palette. Then move the cursor to the location where you want to insert the function and choose the function from the function list.

✦ You can use the Formula Palette to edit a function in an existing formula. Click the Edit Formula button (=) to bring up the Formula Palette. Then click the function in the formula. Use the Formula Palette to adjust the function's arguments.

Using Names

Excel enables you to provide names for cells and ranges. Using names offers the following advantages:

✦ A meaningful range name (such as Total_Income) is much easier to remember than a cell address (such as AC21).

✦ You can quickly move to areas of your worksheet by using the Name box, located at the left side of the formula bar (click the arrow to drop down a list of defined names) or by choosing the Edit➪Go To command (or F5) and specifying the range name.

✦ When you select a named cell or range, the name appears in the Name box.

✦ Creating formulas is easier. You can paste a cell or range name into a formula by using the Insert➪Name➪Paste command or by selecting a name from the Name box.

✦ Names make your formulas more understandable and easier to use. =Income–Taxes is more intuitive than =D20–D40.

✦ Macros are easier to create and maintain when you use range names rather than cell addresses.

Although Excel is quite flexible about the names that you can define, it does have some rules:

✦ Names must begin with a letter or the underscore character (_).

✦ Names can't contain any spaces. You may want to use an underscore or a period character to simulate a space (such as Annual_Total or Annual.Total).

✦ You can use any combination of letters and numbers, but the name must not begin with a number (such as 3rdQuarter) or look like a cell reference (such as Q3).

✦ Most symbols aren't allowed. However, you can use under-score (_), period (.), backslash (\), and question mark (?).

✦ Names are limited to 255 characters.

✦ You can use single letters (except for R or C), but I don't recommend this because it defeats the purpose of using meaningful names.

Remember: A cell or range can have more than one name, there-fore you cannot override the name of a cell or range by typing in a new name.

Excel also uses a few names internally for its own use. Avoid using the following for names: Print_Area, Print_Titles, Consolidate_Area, and Sheet_Title.

Applying names to existing cell references

When you create a new name for a cell or a range, Excel doesn't automatically use the name in place of existing references in your formulas. For example, if you have a formula such as +A1*20 and then give a name to cell A1, the formula continues to display A1 (not the new name). However, it's fairly easy to replace cell or range references with their corresponding names.

To apply names to cell references in existing formulas, follow these steps:

1. Select the range that you want to modify.

2. Choose the Insert⇨Name⇨Apply command.

3. In the Apply Names dialog box, select the names that you want to apply by clicking them.

4. Click OK.

Excel replaces the range references with the names in the selected cells.

If you select a non-formula cell in Step 1, the names are applied to all formulas in the worksheet.

Changing names

Excel doesn't have a simple way to change a name after it's created. If you create a name and then realize that it's not the name you want (or, perhaps, that you spelled it incorrectly), you can change the name by following these steps:

1. Create the new name, using any of the techniques described in this part.

2. Delete the old name.

See also "Deleting names," "Creating names automatically," "Creating names with the Define Name dialog box," and "Creating names using the Name box," all in this part.

Creating names automatically

Your worksheet may contain text that you want to use for names of adjacent cells or ranges. For example, you may have sales region names in column A and corresponding sales figures in column B. You can create a name for each cell in column B by using the text in column A.

To create names using adjacent text, follow these steps:

1. Select the name text and the cells that you want to name (these can be individual cells or ranges of cells).

The names must be adjacent to the cells you're naming (a multiple selection is not allowed here).

2. Choose the Insert⇨Name⇨Create command (or Ctrl+Shift+F3).

Excel guesses how to create the names.

3. Adjust the check boxes in the Create Names dialog box (if necessary) to correspond to the manner in which you want to create the names.

4. Click OK to create the names.

Remember: If the text contained in a cell results in an invalid name, Excel modifies the name to make it valid. If Excel encounters a value or a formula where text should be, however, it doesn't convert it to a valid name. It simply doesn't create a name.

Creating names using the Name box

The Name box is a drop-down list at the extreme left of the formula bar. To create a name using the Name box, follow these steps:

1. Select the cell or range to name.

2. Click the Name box and enter the name.

3. Press Enter to create the name.

Remember: If a name already exists, you can't use the Name box to change the reference that the name refers to. Attempting to do so simply selects the name that you enter.

Creating names with the Define Name dialog box

To create a range name using the Define Name dialog box, follow these steps:

1. Select the cell or range that you want to name.

2. Choose the Insert⇨Name⇨Define command (or press Ctrl+F3).

Excel displays the Define Name dialog box.

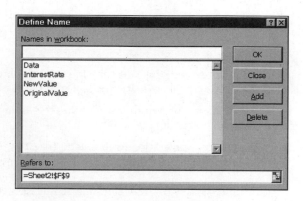

3. Type a name in the edit box labeled Names in workbook (or use the name that Excel proposes, if any).

The active or selected cell or range address appears in the Refers to text box.

4. Verify that the address listed is correct and then click OK to add the name to your worksheet.

5. Click OK to close the dialog box.

Or you can click the Add button to continue adding names to your worksheet. If you do this, you must specify the Refers to range by typing an address (make sure to begin with an equal sign) or by pointing to it in the worksheet. Each name appears in the list box.

Creating a table of names

You may want to create a list of all names in the workbook. This may be useful for tracking down errors or as a way to document your work.

To create a table of names, follow these steps:

1. Move the cell pointer to an empty area of your worksheet (the table will be created at the active cell position).

2. Choose the Insert⇨Name⇨Paste command (or press F3).

3. Click the Paste List button in the Paste Name dialog box.

The list that Excel pastes overwrites any cells that get in the way, so make sure that the active cell is located in an empty portion of the worksheet.

Deleting names

If you no longer need a defined name, you can delete it by following these steps:

1. Choose the Insert⇨Name⇨Define command.

2. In the Define Name dialog box, select the name that you want to delete from the list.

3. Click the Delete button.

Be extra careful when deleting names. If the name is used in a formula, deleting the name causes the formula to become invalid (it will display #NAME?). Even worse, deleting a name can't be undone. It's a good practice to save your workbook before you delete any names.

Remember: If you delete the rows or columns that contain named cells or ranges, the names contain an invalid reference. For example, if cell A1 on Sheet1 is named Interest and you delete row 1 or column A, Interest then refers to =Sheet1!#REF! (that is, an erroneous reference). If you use the name Interest in a formula, the formula displays #REF.

Naming constants

Names that you use in Excel don't need to refer to a cell or range. You can give a name to a constant. For example, if formulas in your worksheet refer to an interest rate (such as .085, or 8.5%) you can define a name for this particular constant and then use it in your formulas.

To define a name for a constant, follow these steps:

1. Choose the Insert⇨Name⇨Define command (or press Ctrl+F3).

Excel displays the Define Name dialog box.

2. Type the name for the constant in the edit box labeled Names in workbook (or use the name that Excel proposes, if any).

3. In the Refers to box, enter the value for the constant. Normally, this field holds a cell or range reference, but you can enter a value (or even a formula) in this box.

4. Click OK to close the dialog box.

After performing these steps, you can use the name in your formulas.

Redefining names

After you define a name, you may want to change the cell or range to which it refers:

1. Select the Insert⇨Name⇨Define command.

2. In the Define Name dialog box, select the name that you want to change.

3. Edit the cell or range address in the Refers to edit box.

If you like, you can click the edit box and select a new cell or range by pointing in the worksheet.

Using multisheet names

Names can extend into the third dimension — across multiple worksheets in a workbook. To create a multisheet name, follow these steps:

1. Choose the Insert⇨Name⇨Define command.

2. Enter the name in the Names in workbook box in the Define Name dialog box.

3. Enter the reference in the Refers to box manually. The format for a multisheet reference is as follows:

```
FirstSheet:LastSheet!RangeReference
```

Remember: This name won't appear in the Name box, however, in the Go To dialog box. Excel lets you define the name, but it doesn't give you a way to automatically select the cells to which the name refers.

Using row and column headers in formulas

You can take advantage of the fact that Excel recognizes row and column headers. You can use these headers to make your formulas more legible. Use the worksheet shown in the following figure as a reference (this workbook doesn't have any defined names).

To refer to a particular cell in this table, you can use the row and column headers (separated by a space). For example, the formula below returns 289:

```
=Feb South
```

If this feature doesn't work, select the Tools⇨Options command and click the Calculation tab. Place a check mark next to the option labeled Accept labels in formulas.

	A	B	C	D	E	F
1		North	South	Total		
2	Jan	132	244	376		
3	Feb	183	289	472		
4	Mar	122	222	344		
5						
6						
7						
8						

Book5 — Sheet1 / Sheet2 \ Sheet3

Remember: This technique only works for formulas that are on the same sheet as the table.

Using sheet level names

Normally, a name that you create can be used anywhere within the workbook. Names, by default, are "book level" names rather than "sheet level" names. But what if you have several worksheets in a workbook and you want to use the same name (such as Dept_Total) on each sheet to signify different values? That's when you need to create sheet level names.

To define a sheet level name, follow these steps:

1. Activate the worksheet where you want to define the name.

2. Choose the Insert⇨Name⇨Define command.

3. In the Names in workbook box, enter the name, but precede it with the worksheet name and an exclamation point. For example, **Sheet2!Dept_Total.**

4. In the Refers to box, enter the cell or range to which the name refers.

You also can create a sheet level name by using the Name box. Select the cell or range, activate the Name box, and enter the name, preceded by the sheet's name and an exclamation point.

Remember: When you write a formula that uses a sheet level name on the sheet where it's defined, you don't need to include the worksheet name in the range name (the Name box doesn't display the worksheet name either). If you use the name in a formula on a different worksheet, however, you must use the entire name (sheet name, exclamation point, and name).

Workbook Auditing

Auditing refers to the process of tracking down and identifying errors in your workbook.

Handling circular references

When you enter formulas, you may occasionally see a message from Excel like the one shown in the following figure. This indicates that the formula you just entered will result in a circular reference.

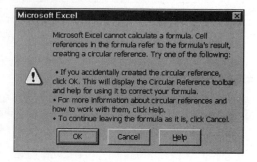

A *circular reference* occurs when a formula refers to its own value (either directly or indirectly).

When you get the circular reference message after entering a formula, Excel displays a message that lets you correct the formula, or enter the formula as it is. If you enter a formula with a circular reference, Excel displays a message in the status bar to remind you that a circular reference exists. Most of the time, a circular reference indicates an error that must be corrected.

To locate the cells in the circular reference, use the Circular Reference toolbar. This toolbar contains a drop-down list that helps you move to each cell in the circular reference so you can change the formulas as needed to correct the error. Excel displays the Circular Reference toolbar (and a help window) automatically when you select OK in the dialog box that displays the message about the circular reference.

Remember: Excel doesn't tell you about a circular reference if the Iteration setting is on. You can check this in the Options dialog box (in the Calculation panel). If Iteration is on, Excel performs the circular calculation the number of times specified in the Maximum Iterations field (or until the value changes by less than .001 — or whatever value is in the Maximum change field).

A few situations exist (known about by advanced users) in which you would use a circular reference intentionally. In these cases, the Iteration setting must be on. It's best, however, to keep the Iteration setting off so that Excel warns you of circular references.

Using Excel's auditing tools

Excel provides a set of interactive auditing tools that you may find helpful. You can access these tools by using Tools⇨Auditing (which results in a submenu with additional choices) or from the Auditing toolbar (to display the Auditing toolbar select Tools⇨ Auditing⇨Show Auditing Toolbar).

The tools on the Auditing toolbar are as follows:

Trace Precedents: Draws arrows to indicate a formula cell's precedents. (A precedent cell supplies the values in a formula.) You can click this multiple times to see additional levels of precedents.

Remove Precedent Arrows: Removes the most recently placed set of precedent arrows.

Trace Dependents: Draws arrows to indicate a cell's dependents. (A dependent cell is a formula cell that depends on another cell.) You can click this multiple times to see additional levels of dependents.

Remove Dependent Arrows: Removes the most recently placed set of dependent arrows.

Remove All Arrows: Removes all precedent and dependent arrows from the worksheet.

Trace Error: Draws arrows from a cell that contains an error to the cells that may have caused the error.

New Comment: Inserts a Cell Comment for the active cell. This doesn't have much to do with auditing — it just lets you attach a comment to a cell.

Circle Invalid Data: Draws a circle around cells that contain invalid data. These are cells that contain validation criteria set by the Data⇨Validation command.

 Clear Validation Circles: Removes the circles from cells that contain invalid data.

These tools can identify precedents and dependents by drawing arrows (known as *cell tracers*) on the worksheet.

Remember: *Precedents* are cells that are referred to by a formula (either directly or indirectly). *Dependents* are formulas that depend on a particular cell.

Excel also has some shortcut keys that you can use to select precedents and dependents.

Key Combination	What It Selects
Ctrl+[	Direct precedents
Ctrl+Shift+[	All precedents
Ctrl+]	Direct dependents
Ctrl+Shift+]	All dependents

 If you're not inclined to remember shortcut key combinations, you can select precedents and dependents by choosing the Edit⇨Go To command and clicking the Special button in the Go To dialog box.

Viewing formulas

One way to audit your workbook is to display the formulas rather than the results of the formulas. Then you can examine the formulas without having to scroll through the worksheet. To do this, follow these steps:

1. Select the Tools⇨Options command.

2. Click the View tab of the Options dialog box.

3. Check the box labeled Formulas under Window options.

 You may want to create a new window for the workbook before issuing this command. That way, you can see the formulas in one window and the results in the other.

Part VI

Analyzing Spreadsheet Data

Much of what you do with Excel involves analyzing data. This part deals with a variety of topics related to data analysis.

In this part . . .

✔ **Managing lists of data maintained in a worksheet**

✔ **Sorting and filtering lists**

✔ **Accessing data stored in external database files**

✔ **Using goal seeking**

✔ **Performing what-if analysis**

✔ **Creating data tables**

✔ **Using the Excel scenario management tools**

✔ **Using pivot tables**

✔ **Using the Analysis ToolPak add-in**

Filtering and Sorting Lists

You can store information of just about any type in a *list*. If you're familiar with the concept of a *database table,* you'll recognize that a list has many similarities:

✦ Columns correspond to fields.

✦ Rows correspond to records.

✦ The first row of the table should have field names that describe the data in each column.

Use Window⇨Freeze Panes to make sure that the headings are always visible when the list is scrolled.

See also "Freezing row or column titles," in Part II.

You can preformat entire columns to ensure that the data will have the same format. For example, if a column contains dates, format the entire column with the desired date format.

Excel 2000 comes with a new feature, List AutoFill, which is turned on by default. The List AutoFill feature automatically copies formatting and formulas when new rows are added below the last row in the list. You can toggle this feature by selecting the Tools⇨Options command, clicking the Edit tab, and checking or clearing the Extend list formats and formulas check box.

Remember: An Excel worksheet has 65,536 rows, and a cell can hold more than 32,000 characters.

See also "Using Data Entry Forms," in Part IV.

Applying database functions with lists

To create a formula that returns results based on filtered criteria, use the Excel database worksheet functions. For example, you can create a formula that calculates the sum of values in a list that meet certain criteria. Set up a criteria range in your worksheet and then enter a formula such as the following:

```
=DSUM(ListRange,FieldName,Criteria)
```

In this case, *ListRange* refers to the list, *FieldName* refers to the field name cell of the column being summed, and *Criteria* refers to the criteria range.

The following table describes the Excel database functions.

Function	Description
DAVERAGE	Returns the average of selected database entries
DCOUNT	Counts the cells containing numbers from a specified database and criteria
DCOUNTA	Counts nonblank cells from a specified database and criteria
DGET	Extracts from a database a single record that matches the specified criteria
DMAX	Returns the maximum value from selected database entries
DMIN	Returns the minimum value from selected database entries
DPRODUCT	Multiplies the values in a particular field of records that match the criteria in a database
DSTDEV	Estimates the standard deviation based on a sample of selected database entries
DSTDEVP	Calculates the standard deviation based on the entire population of selected database entries
DSUM	Adds the numbers in the field column of records in the database that match the criteria
DVAR	Estimates variance based on a sample from selected database entries
DVARP	Calculates variance based on the entire population of selected database entries

See also "Setting up a criteria range for advanced filtering," in this part, and "Using the Formula Palette to enter functions," in Part V.

The following table shows examples of text criteria.

Criteria	Effect
>K	Text that begins with L through Z
<>C	All text, except text that begins with C
January	Text that matches January
Sm*	Text that begins with sm
s*s	Text that begins with s and ends with s
s?s	Three-letter text that begins with *s* and ends with *s*

Remember: The text comparisons are not case sensitive. For example, si* matches *Simon* as well as *sick*.

Computed criteria filters the list based on one or more calculations and does not use a field header from the list (it uses a new field header). Computed criteria essentially computes a new field for the list so that you must supply new field names in the first row of the criteria range.

Computed criteria is a logical formula (returns True or False) that refers to cells in the first row of data in the list; it does *not* refer to the header row.

Filtering a list with autofiltering

Autofiltering lets you view only certain rows in your list by hiding rows that do not qualify based on criteria you set.

To autofilter a list, follow these steps:

1. Move the cell pointer anywhere within the list.

2. Choose the Data⇨Filter⇨AutoFilter command.

Excel analyzes your list and then adds drop-down arrows to the field names in the header row.

	A	B	C	D	E	F
1	**Month**	**Sales Rep**	**Type**	**Unit Cost**	**Quantit**	**Total Sale**
2	January	Franks	Existing	175	5	875
3	January	Franks	Existing	175	1	175
4	February	Franks	Existing	225	1	225
5	March	Franks	Existing	125	2	250
6	March	Franks	Existing	125	4	500
7	April	Franks	New	175	4	700
8	April	Franks	New	175	3	525
9	April	Franks	Existing	125	1	125
10	April	Franks	Existing	125	1	125
11	May	Franks	New	140	3	420
12	May	Franks	Existing	125	1	125
13	January	Jenkins	Existing	125	1	125
14	January	Jenkins	Existing	175	2	350
15	January	Jenkins	New	140	1	140
16	February	Jenkins	New	225	3	675

SalesReport2.xls

PivotTable \ SALES-DB

3. Click the arrow on one of these drop-down lists.

The list expands to show the unique items in that column.

4. Select an item.

Excel hides all rows except those that include the selected item. In other words, the list is filtered by the item that you selected.

Remember: After you filter the list, the status bar displays a message that tells you how many rows qualified. In addition, the drop-down arrow changes color to remind you that the list is filtered by a value in that column.

The drop-down list includes five other items:

All: Displays all items in the column. Use this to remove filtering for a column.

Top 10: Filters to display the "top 10" items in the list. Actually, you can display any number of the top (or bottom) values.

Custom: Lets you filter the list by multiple items.

Blanks: Filters the list by showing only rows that contain blanks in this column.

NonBlanks: Filters the list by showing only rows that contain non-blanks in this column.

The Blanks and NonBlanks options will only appear if the list contains at least one blank field.

To display the entire list again, select the Data⇨Filter⇨Show All command.

To get out of AutoFilter mode and remove the drop-down arrows from the field names, choose the Data⇨Filter⇨AutoFilter command again.

See also "Performing advanced filtering" and "Filtering a list with custom autofiltering," both in this part.

Filtering a list with custom autofiltering

Normally, autofiltering involves selecting a single value for one or more columns. The list is then filtered by that value. For more flexibility, choose the Custom option in an AutoFilter drop-down list.

The Custom AutoFilter dialog box lets you filter in several ways:

✦ **Values above or below a specified value:** For example, sales amounts GREATER THAN 10,000.

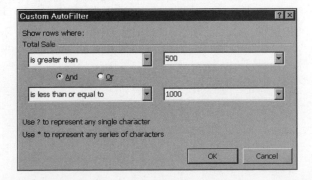

✦ **Values within a range:** For example, sales amounts greater than 10,000 AND sales amounts less than 50,000.

✦ **Values outside of a range:** For example, sales amounts LESS THAN 10,000 or sales amounts greater than 50,000.

✦ **Two discrete values:** For example, state equal to New York OR state equal to New Jersey.

✦ **Approximate matches:** You can use the * and ? wildcards to filter in many other ways. For example, to display only those customers whose last name begins with a B, use **B***.

Custom autofiltering is useful, but it has limitations. For example, if you would like to filter the list to show only three values in a field (such as New York or New Jersey or Connecticut), you can't do it by using autofiltering. Such filtering tasks require the advanced filtering feature.

See also "Performing advanced filtering," in this part.

Performing advanced filtering

Advanced filtering is more flexible than autofiltering, but it takes some up-front work to use it. Advanced filtering provides you with the following capabilities:

✦ You can specify more complex filtering criteria.

✦ You can specify computed filtering criteria.

✦ You can extract a copy of the rows that meet the criteria to another location.

To perform advanced filtering on a list, follow these steps:

1. Set up a criteria range.

2. Choose the Data⇨Filter⇨Advanced Filter command.

3. In the Advanced Filter dialog box, specify the list range and the criteria range, and make sure to select the option labeled Filter the list, in-place.

4. Click OK, and the list is filtered by the criteria that you specified.

See also "Setting up a criteria range for advanced filtering," in this part.

Setting up a criteria range for advanced filtering

Before you can use the advanced filtering feature, you must set up a *criteria range* — a range on a worksheet that holds the information Excel uses to filter the list. The criteria range must conform to the following specifications:

✦ The criteria range consists of at least two rows.

✦ The first row contains some or all of the field names from the list.

✦ The other rows consist of filtering criteria.

If you use more than one row below the field names in the criteria range, the criteria in each row are joined with an OR operator.

The entries that you make in a criteria range can be either of the following:

✦ Text or value criteria: The filtering involves comparisons to a value or text, using operators such as equal (=), greater than (>), not equal to (<>), and so on.

✦ Computed criteria: The filtering involves some sort of computation.

Sorting a list

Sorting a list involves rearranging the rows such that they are in ascending or descending order, based on the values in one or more columns. For example, you might want to sort a list of salespeople alphabetically by last name or by sales region. The fastest way to sort a list is to use the Sort Ascending or Sort Descending buttons on the Standard toolbar:

1. Move the cell pointer to the column upon which you want to base the sort.

2. Click the Sort Ascending button or the Sort Descending button.

Excel sorts the list by the current column.

You may need to sort a list by more than one column. For example, you might want to sort by state, by city within the state, and by zip code within the city. To sort a list on multiple columns, use the procedure above for each column that you want to sort. Always start with the "least important" column (for example, zip code) and end with the "most important" column (for example, state).

When you sort a filtered list, only the visible rows are sorted. When you remove the filtering from the list, the list will no longer be sorted.

If the sorted list contains formulas that refer to cells in other rows in the list, the formulas will not be correct after the sorting. If formulas in your list refer to cells outside the list, make sure that the formulas use an absolute cell reference.

Another way to sort a list follows:

1. Choose the Data⇨Sort command.

Excel displays the Sort dialog box.

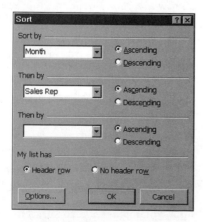

2. Select the first sort field from the drop-down list labeled Sort by and specify Ascending or Descending order.

3. Repeat Step 2 for the second and third sort fields (if desired).

4. Click Options and select any sort options (described below).

- **First key sort order:** Lets you specify a custom sort order for the sort.

- **Case sensitive:** Makes the sorting case sensitive so that uppercase letters appear before lowercase letters in an ascending sort. Normally, sorting ignores the case of letters.

- **Orientation:** Lets you sort by columns rather than by rows (the default).

5. Click OK to return to the Sort dialog box.

6. Click OK and the list's rows are rearranged.

Remember: If the Header row option is set, the first row (field names) is not affected by the sort.

Sorting a list by more than three fields requires an additional step. If you want to sort your list by five fields (Field1, Field2, Field3, Field4, and Field5), start with sorting by Field3, Field4, and Field5. Then re-sort the list by Field1 and Field2. In other words, sort the three "least important" fields first; they remain in sequence when you do the second sort.

Often, you'll want to keep the records in their original order but perform a temporary sort just to see how the rearranged data looks. To perform a temporary sort, add an additional column to the list with sequential numbers in it. Then, after you sort, you can return to the original order by re-sorting on the field that has the sequential numbers. You can also use the Edit⇨Undo command to reverse the effects of sorting.

See also "Using a custom sort order," in this part.

Using a custom sort order

Sorting is done either numerically or alphabetically, depending on the data. In some cases, you may want to sort your data in other ways. If your data consists of month names, you probably want them to appear in month order rather than alphabetically. Excel, by default, has four custom lists, and you can define your own. To sort by a custom list, click the Options button in the Sort dialog box; then select the list from the First key sort order drop-down list.

Excel custom lists are as follows:

✦ **Abbreviated days:** Sun, Mon, Tue, Wed, Thu, Fri, Sat

✦ **Days:** Sunday, Monday, Tuesday, Wednesday, Thursday, Friday, Saturday

✦ **Abbreviated months:** Jan, Feb, Mar, Apr, May, Jun, Jul, Aug, Sep, Oct, Nov, Dec

✦ **Months:** January, February, March, April, May, June, July, August, September, October, November, December

To create a custom list, follow these steps:

1. Choose the Tools⇨Options command.

2. In the Options dialog box, click the Custom Lists tab.

3. Click the NEW LIST option.

4. Enter your list in the List entries box.

5. Click Add and then click OK to close the Options dialog box.

Using an external database

Accessing external database files from Excel is useful when

✦ The database that you need to work with is very large.

✦ The database is shared with others; that is, other users have access to the database and may need to work with the data at the same time.

✦ You want to work with only a subset of the data that meets certain criteria.

✦ The database is in a format that Excel can't read.

After you bring the data into Excel, you can manipulate and format it using any of the Excel commands.

To work with an external database file from Excel, you use the *Microsoft Query* application (which is included with Excel and must be installed).

If a query has already been defined, use the Data⇨Get External Data⇨Run Saved Query command. Select a query from the Run Query dialog box. You can then specify what to do with the returned data.

The general procedure for creating a new database query is as follows:

1. Activate a worksheet.

2. Choose the <u>D</u>ata⇨Get External <u>D</u>ata⇨<u>N</u>ew Database Query command.

The Microsoft Query application starts up.

3. In Microsoft Query, you select the database that you want to use.

4. The Query Wizard walks you through the steps required to create the query.

5. In the final step of the Query Wizard, specify what you want to do with the returned data. You can return the data to your worksheet, or view the data in Microsoft Query.

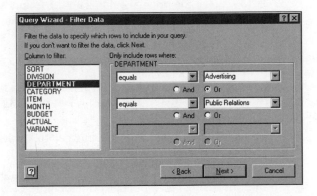

If you choose to return the data to your worksheet, the records that meet your criteria are copied to the worksheet, where you can do whatever you like with the data.

Goal Seeking: Making a Formula Return a Desired Value

Excel's goal-seeking feature lets you determine the value that a single input cell requires to produce a result that you want in a dependent (formula) cell. Here's the procedure:

1. Start with a workbook that uses formulas.

2. Select the <u>T</u>ools⇨<u>G</u>oal Seek command.

3. Complete the Goal Seek dialog box by specifying the formula cell to change, the value to change it to, and the cell to change.

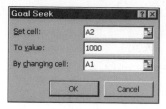

4. Click OK.

Excel displays the solution.

5. Click OK to replace the original value with the found value; or click Cancel to restore your worksheet to the form that it was in before you issued the Tools⇨Goal Seek command.

Remember: Excel can't always find a value that produces the result you're looking for (sometimes a solution doesn't exist). In such a case, the Goal Seek status box informs you of that fact. If Excel reports that it can't find a solution, but you're pretty sure that one exists, try these options:

✦ Change the current value of the changing cell to a value closer to the solution and then reissue the command.

✦ Adjust the Maximum iterations setting in the Calculation panel of the Options dialog box (Tools⇨Options). Increasing the number of iterations makes Excel try other possible solutions.

✦ Double-check your logic and make sure that the formula cell does indeed depend on the specified changing cell.

Performing What-If Analysis (Scenarios)

What-if analysis refers to the process of changing one or more input cells and observing the effects on formulas. An *input cell* is a cell that is used by a formula. For example, if a formula calculates a monthly payment amount for a loan, the formula would refer to an input cell that contains the loan amount.

Creating a data table (one-input)

A *one-input data table* displays the results of one or more result formulas for multiple values of a single input cell. For example, if you have a formula that calculates a loan payment, you can create a data table that shows the payment amount for various interest rates. The interest rate cell is the input cell.

Values of the single input cell

Not used   Any number of formulas or references to formulas

Results of the 1-input table
(in any array formula)

The following table describes how the one-input data table is set up:

Table Area	Description
Left column	Values for the single input cell
Top row	Formulas or references to result formulas elsewhere in the worksheet
Upper-left cell	Not used
Remaining cells	Results entered by Excel

To create the table, follow these steps:

1. Select the table range.

2. Choose the Data⇨Table command.

3. Specify the worksheet cell that you're using as the input value.

   If the variables for the input cell are located in a column, use the Column input cell field. If the variables are in a row, use the Row input cell field.

4. Click OK.

   Excel performs the calculations and fills in the table.

Remember: Excel uses an array formula that uses the TABLE function. Therefore, the table will be updated if you change the cell references in the first row or plug in different values in the first column.

See also "Creating a data table (two-input)," in this part.

Creating a data table (two-input)

A *two-input data table* displays the results of a single formula for various values of *two*-input cells. For example, if you have a formula that calculates a loan payment, you can create a data table that shows the payment amount for various interest rates and loan amounts. The interest rate cell and the loan amount cell are the input cells.

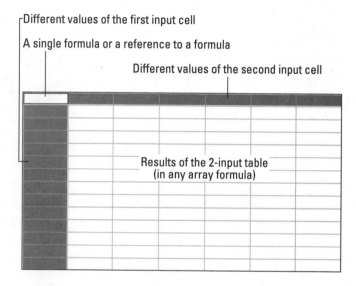

Different values of the first input cell

A single formula or a reference to a formula

Different values of the second input cell

Results of the 2-input table
(in any array formula)

The following table describes how the two-input data table is set up:

Table Area	Description
Left column	Values for the first input cell
Top row	Values for the second input cell
Upper-left cell	Reference to the single result formula
Remaining cells	Results entered by Excel

To create a two-input data table, follow these steps:

1. Select the table range.

2. Choose the Data⇨Table command.

3. Specify the cell for the Row input cell.

4. Specify the cell for the Column input cell.

5. Click OK.

Excel performs the calculations and fills in the table.

See also "Creating a data table (one-input)," in this part.

Creating a named scenario

The Excel scenario manager feature lets you store different sets of input values (called *changing cells*) for any number of variables and gives a name to each set. You can then select a set of values by name, and Excel displays the worksheet using those values.

To define a scenario, follow these steps:

1. Create your worksheet as usual, using input cells that determine the result of one or more formulas.

2. Choose the Tools⇨Scenarios command to display the Scenario Manager dialog box.

3. In the Scenario Manager dialog box, click the Add button to add a scenario.

4. Complete the Add Scenario dialog box (the settings are described as follows).

- **Scenario name:** The name for the scenario. You can give it any name that you like.

- **Changing cells:** The input cells for the scenario. You can enter the cell addresses directly or point to them. Multiple selections are allowed, so the input cells do not need to be adjacent. Each named scenario can use the same set of changing cells or different changing cells.

- **Comment:** By default, Excel displays who created the scenario and the date it was created. You can change this text, add new text to it, or delete it altogether.

- **Protection:** The two options (protecting a scenario and hiding a scenario) are in effect only when the worksheet is protected and the Scenarios option is chosen in the Protect Sheet dialog box. Protecting a scenario prevents anyone from modifying it; a hidden scenario doesn't appear in the Scenario Manager dialog box.

5. Click OK to display the Scenario Values dialog box.

6. Enter the values for this scenario in the Scenario Values dialog box.

7. Click the Add button to add the scenario.

8. Repeat Steps 4 through 7 for each additional scenario.

9. Click Close to close the Scenario Manager dialog box.

It's excellent practice to create names for the changing cells, because names make the cells easier to identify in the Scenario Values dialog box. Names also help make scenario reports more readable.

Remember: The number of changing cells for a scenario is limited to 32.

See also "Creating a scenario summary report," in this part.

Creating a scenario summary report

After you've defined at least two scenarios, you can generate reports that summarize the scenarios by following these steps:

1. Choose the Tools⇨Scenarios command.

2. Click the Summary button in the Scenario Manager dialog box.

3. Select the type of report (described as follows).

- **Scenario summary:** The summary report is in the form of an outline.

- **Scenario PivotTable:** The summary report is in the form of a pivot table. This gives you more flexibility if you have many scenarios defined with multiple result cells.

4. In the Result cells box, specify the summary cells to include in the report and then click OK.

Excel creates a new worksheet to store the summary table.

It's excellent practice to create names for the result cells, because Excel uses these names in the scenario summary reports you create. The names help make your reports more readable.

See also "Creating a named scenario" and "Pivot Tables," in this part.

Displaying a named scenario

When you view a scenario, Excel inserts the scenario's values into the change cells. Formulas that depend on these cells will be updated. To view a named scenario, follow these steps:

1. Select the Tools⇨Scenarios command.

2. Select the scenario from the list and click Show.

You can view as many scenarios as you like while the Scenario Manager dialog box is displayed. When you're finished, click Close. Values for the last scenario viewed will remain in the worksheet.

Pivot Tables

A *pivot table* is a dynamic summary of data contained in a database (contained on a worksheet or in an external file). A pivot table lets you create frequency distributions and cross-tabulations of several different data dimensions. In addition, you can display subtotals and any level of detail you desire.

Generally speaking, fields in a database table can be one of two types:

◆ Data: Contains a value

◆ Category: Describes the data

A database table can have any number of data fields and any number of category fields. When you create a pivot table, you usually want to summarize one or more of the data fields. The values in the category fields appear in the pivot table as rows, columns, or pages.

Creating a pivot table

To create a pivot table from a worksheet database, follow these steps:

1. Move the cell pointer to any cell in the database.

2. Choose the Data⇔PivotTable and PivotChart Report command.

Excel displays the first of three dialog boxes.

3. Make sure that the options labeled Microsoft Excel List or Database and PivotTable are selected and click Next.

4. In the second dialog box, ensure that the database range is specified (Excel automatically identifies the database range) and click Next.

5. In the third dialog box, specify the location for the pivot table (a new worksheet or an existing worksheet).

6. Click the Options button if desired to specify additional options (see below) and then click Finish.

7. Excel 2000 displays on-sheet interactive drop zones and a floating PivotTable Toolbar that includes the field names from your database. Drag the field names from the PivotTable toolbar to the appropriate drop zones. The drop zones are outlined in blue and are labeled for easy identification.

Excel creates the pivot table.

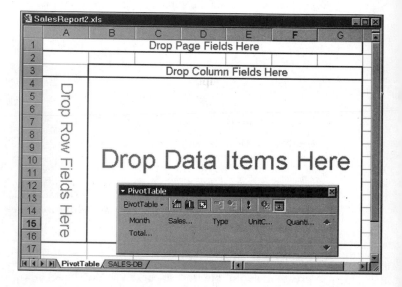

Excel includes several options for pivot tables, which are available when you click the <u>O</u>ptions button in the third step of the PivotTable Wizard. The following text describes these options.

<u>A</u>utoFormat table: Check this box if you want Excel to apply a default AutoFormat to the pivot table. Excel uses the AutoFormat even if you rearrange the table layout.

Subtotal <u>h</u>idden page items: Check this box if you want Excel to include hidden items in the Page fields in the subtotals.

<u>M</u>erge labels: Check this box if you want Excel to merge the cells for outer row and column labels. Doing so may make the table more readable.

<u>P</u>reserve formatting: Check this box if you would like Excel to keep any formatting that you applied when the pivot table is updated.

Repeat item labels on each printed page: Check this box if you want Excel to repeat item labels on each page for all rows to the left of the field for which a page break separates a group of items.

Page layout: Specify the order in which you want the page fields to appear.

Fields per column: Specify the number of page fields to show before starting another row of page fields.

For error values, show: You can specify a value to show for pivot table cells that display an error.

For empty cells, show: You can specify a value to show for pivot table cells that are empty.

Set print titles: Check this box if you want Excel to repeat row labels, column labels, and item labels on each page of a PivotTable report. This option is applicable only for PivotTable reports in indented format (*see* "Formatting a pivot table" in this part). Also, Page Setup options used to repeat rows and columns should be cleared.

Save data with table layout: If this option is checked, Excel stores an additional copy of the data (called a *pivot table cache*) to allow it to recalculate the table more quickly when you change the layout. If memory is an issue, keep this option unchecked (updating will be a bit slower).

Enable drilldown: If checked, you can double-click a cell in the pivot table to view details.

Refresh on open: If checked, the pivot table is refreshed whenever you open the workbook.

Refresh every xxxxx minutes: To periodically refresh a report based on external data, check this box and then enter the interval you want in the minutes box. This check box is unavailable for reports based on Excel source data. Minutes can range from 1 to 32767 inclusive.

Save password: If you use an external database that requires a password, this option enables you to store the password as part of the query so you won't have to enter it.

Background query: If checked, Excel runs the external database query in the background while you continue your work.

Optimize memory: This option reduces the amount of memory used when you refresh an external database query.

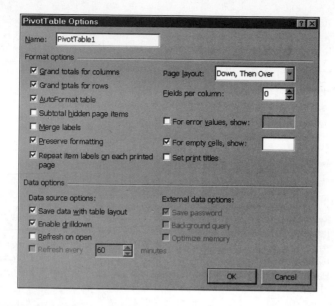

If the data is in an external database, select the External Data Source option in Step 3, of the preceding list of steps. The data is retrieved using MS Query (a separate application), and you'll be prompted for the data source in the second PivotTable Wizard dialog box.

See also "Using an external database," in this part.

Remember: In Step 7, you can drag as many fields as you want to any of the drop zones, and you don't have to use all the fields. Fields that aren't used don't appear in the pivot table.

Formatting a pivot table

When you create a pivot table, you have an option of applying a default table AutoFormat. After the pivot table is created, you can specify a different AutoFormat. Excel 2000 comes with a new PivotTable AutoFormat feature that provides 22 pivot table AutoFormats.

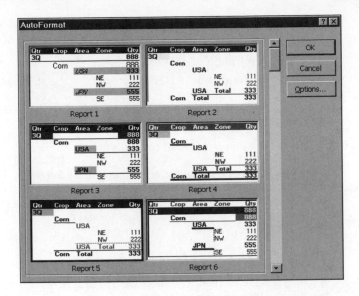

To change or use an AutoFormat after the pivot table is created, select a cell within the pivot table and use any of the these methods:

◆ Choose the Format⇨AutoFormat command. This command displays the AutoFormat dialog box with a list of pivot table AutoFormats. This list replaces the standard worksheet AutoFormats.

◆ Right-click anywhere in the pivot table and select Format Report from the shortcut menu.

◆ Choose the PivotTable⇨Format Report command on the Pivot Table toolbar.

When Excel creates a pivot table report, it does not retain any special number formatting that you may have applied to your original data. For example, if you apply a currency format to your data and then use that data in the pivot table, the currency formatting is not retained in the pivot table.

To change the number format for the data in the pivot table, here's
what you need to do:

1. Select any cell in the pivot table's data area.

2. Right-click and choose Field Settings from the shortcut menu.

Excel displays its PivotTable Field dialog box.

3. Click the Number button.

4. Select the number format that you need.

Remember: Use one of the AutoFormats labeled Report 1, Report 2,
Report 3, and so on when you want to display and/or print a report
in indented format, similar to the traditional banded or formatted
database report. Selecting an indented format changes the layout of
your report.

Grouping pivot table items

A handy feature enables you to group specific items in a field of a
pivot table. If one of the fields in your database consists of dates,
for example, the pivot table displays a separate row or column for
every date. You may find it more useful to group the dates into
months or quarters and then hide the details.

To create a group of items in a pivot table, follow these steps:

1. Select the cells to be grouped.

2. Choose the Data⇨Group and Outline⇨Group command.

Excel creates a new field that consists of the selected items.

3. You can change the names of the new field and the items by
editing them in the Formula bar.

If the items to be grouped are not next to each other, make a
multiple selection by pressing Ctrl and selecting the items that will
make up the group.

If the field items consist of values, dates, or times, you can let
Excel do the grouping for you. To create groups *automatically,*
follow these steps:

1. Select any item in the field (only one).

2. Choose the <u>D</u>ata⇨<u>G</u>roup and Outline⇨<u>G</u>roup command.

Excel displays the Grouping dialog box.

3. Select the grouping options.

4. Click OK.

Excel creates the groups.

Inserting a calculated field into a pivot table

Excel lets you create new calculated fields for a pivot table. For example, if you have a field named TotalSales, you may want to create a calculated field to project sales for another period. The calculation would use the value of TotalSales. Calculated fields must reside in the Data area of the pivot table (you cannot use them in the Page, Row, or Column areas).

To create a calculated field, follow these steps:

1. Move the cell pointer anywhere within the pivot table.

2. Right-click and choose For<u>m</u>ulas⇨Calculated <u>F</u>ield from the shortcut menu.

Excel displays the Insert Calculated Field dialog box.

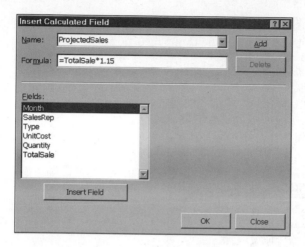

3. Enter a name for the field and specify the formula. The formula can use other fields and worksheet functions, but it cannot refer to cells or use names.

4. Click the Add button.

5. Repeat Steps 3 and 4 if you want to create additional fields.

6. Click OK to close the dialog box.

After you create the field, it appears in the pivot table.

Remember: If you plan on using field names in your calculated field formulas, you should name the fields without spaces.

Inserting a calculated item into a pivot table

Excel enables you to create new calculated items for a pivot table. For example, if you have a field named Months, you can create a calculated item (called Q1, for example) that displays the sum of January, February, and March. Calculated items must reside in the Page, Row, or Column area of a pivot table (you cannot use them in the Data area).

To create a calculated item, follow these steps:

1. Move the cell pointer to a Row, Column, or Page area of the pivot table.

The cell pointer cannot be in the Data area.

2. Right-click and choose Formulas➪Calculated Item from the shortcut menu.

Excel displays the Insert Calculated Item dialog box.

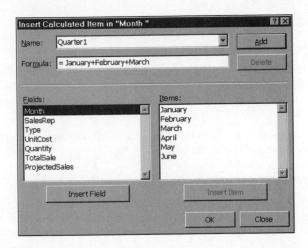

3. Type a name for the item and specify the formula.

The formula can use items in other fields and worksheet functions, but it cannot refer to cells or use names.

4. Click the <u>A</u>dd button.

5. Repeat Steps 3 and 4 if you want to create additional items.

6. Click OK to close the dialog box.

After you create the item, it appears in the pivot table.

Remember: If you plan on using item names in your calculated item formulas, you should name the items without spaces.

Inserting a new field into a pivot table

To add a new field to a pivot table, follow these steps:

1. Move the cell pointer anywhere within the pivot table.

2. Drag the new field from the PivotTable toolbar to the desired location in the pivot table.

Modifying a pivot table's structure

A pivot table displayed in a worksheet includes the field buttons. You can drag any of the field buttons to a new position in the pivot table (this is known as *pivoting*). For example, you can drag a column field to a row position. Excel immediately redisplays the pivot table to reflect your change.

You also can change the order of the row fields or the column fields by dragging the buttons. This affects how the fields are nested and can have a dramatic effect on how the table looks.

Remember: A pivot table is a special type of range, and (except for formatting) you can't make any changes to it. For example, you can't insert or delete rows, edit results, or move cells. If you attempt to do so, Excel displays an error message.

You can also drag fields from the PivotTable toolbar to modify an existing pivot table's structure.

Refreshing a pivot table

If you change the source data that is used by a pivot table, the pivot table doesn't get updated automatically. Rather, you must *refresh* it manually. To refresh a pivot table, use any of the these methods:

✦ Choose the Data⇨Refresh Data command.

✦ Right-click anywhere in the pivot table and select Refresh Data from the shortcut menu.

✦ Click the Refresh button on the Pivot Table toolbar.

Remember: If the source database is large, there may be some delay while this recalculation takes place, but for small databases the update is virtually instantaneous.

If your pivot table is based on external data, Excel 2000 provides an option to refresh the data automatically every xxxxx minutes, where xxxxx can be any integer from 1 to 32,767 inclusive. Click the Options button in Step 3 of 3 of the PivotTable and PivotChart Wizard, or right-click anywhere in the pivot table and select Table Options from the shortcut menu to access this option.

Removing a field from a pivot table

To remove a field from a pivot table, follow these steps:

1. Click the field button that you want to remove.

2. Drag it away from the pivot table.

3. Release the mouse button, and Excel updates the pivot table, removing the field you dragged away.

Part VII

Charting, Drawing, and Web Publishing

This part deals with topics related to creating charts and publishing for the Web. It also covers the Microsoft Excel 2000 drawing tools, which you can use to draw diagrams directly on a worksheet.

In this part . . .

- Creating and customizing charts
- Using the Excel drawing tools
- Publishing your documents on the WebCharting

Charting

Before you can do anything with a chart, you must activate it:

✦ To activate a chart on a chart sheet, click the chart sheet's tab.

✦ To activate an embedded chart, click the chart.

When you click an embedded chart, you actually select the part that you clicked.

Adding a new data series to a chart

You can add a new data series to a chart in several ways:

✦ Select the range to be added and drag it into the chart. When you release the mouse button, Excel updates the chart with the data you dragged into it. This technique works only if the chart is embedded on the worksheet.

✦ Activate the chart and select the Chart⇨Add Data command. Excel displays a dialog box that prompts you for the range of data to add to the chart.

✦ Select the range to be added and copy it to the Office Clipboard. Then activate the chart and choose the Edit⇨Paste Special command. Excel responds with the Paste Special dialog box. Complete this dialog box to correspond to the data that you selected.

✦ Activate the chart and then click the Chart Wizard tool. You'll get the first Chart Wizard dialog box. Click the Next button to get to the second dialog box. Edit the range reference to include the new data series (or point to the new range in the worksheet). Click Finish and Excel updates the chart with the new data.

Adding a trendline to a data series

When you're plotting data over time, you may want to plot a *trendline* that points out general trends in your data. In some cases, you also can forecast future data with trendlines:

1. Activate the chart.

2. Select the data series.

3. Choose the Chart⇨Add Trendline command.

4. Click the Type tab of Add Trendline dialog box, and choose the type of trendline you want; then click OK.

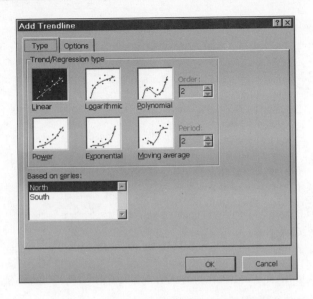

You can also set options by clicking the Options tab.

The Options tab enables you to specify a name to appear in the legend and the number of periods that you want to forecast. Two additional options enable you to specify that the equation used for the trendline and the R^2 value appear on the chart.

Remember: When Excel inserts a trendline, it may look like a new data series, but it's not. The trendline is a new chart element with a name, such as Series 1 Trendline 1. You can double-click a trendline to change its formatting or its options. A series can have more than one trendline.

Remember: You cannot add trendlines to all chart types. If the Chart⇨Add Trendline command is not accessible (for example, the command is grayed out), you cannot add a trendline to the series you chose.

Adding error bars to a data series

For certain chart types, you can add *error bars* to indicate "plus or minus" information that reflects uncertainty in the data. Error bars are appropriate only for area, bar, column, line, and XY charts:

1. Activate the chart.

2. Select the data series.

3. Choose the Format⇨Selected Data Series command (or double-click the series).

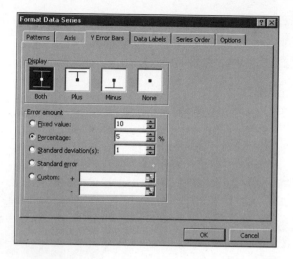

4. In the Format Data Series dialog box, click the Y Error Bars tab.

5. Select the type of error bar you want and then click OK.

The error bar choices are as follows:

✦ **Fixed Value:** The error bars are fixed by an amount you specify.

✦ **Percentage:** The error bars are a percentage of each value.

✦ **Standard deviation(s):** The error bars are in the number of standard deviation units that you specify. (Excel calculates the standard deviation of the data series.)

✦ **Standard error:** The error bars are one standard error unit. (Excel calculates the standard error of the data series.)

✦ **Custom:** You set the error bar units for the upper or lower error bars. You can either enter a value or a range reference that holds the error values that you want to plot as error bars.

Remember: A data series in an XY chart can have error bars for both the X values and Y values.

Adding fill effects to a chart

You can change the fill pattern used in various chart elements to produce dramatic or unusual effects. You can change the fill pattern for the chart area, the plot area, columns, and bars.

To change the fill effects, follow these steps:

1. Double-click the chart element that you want to modify.

Excel displays a dialog box.

2. Select the Patterns tab.

3. Click the F<u>i</u>ll Effects button.

Excel displays the Fill Effects dialog box.

4. Select one of the four tabs (Gradient, Texture, Pattern, or Picture).

5. Specify the type of fill that you want. There are many options, and they are all quite straightforward.

6. Click OK twice to close the dialog boxes.

Changing a chart's data series

Often, you create a chart that uses a particular range of data, and then you extend the data range by adding new data points in the worksheet. When you add new data to a range, the new data won't be included in the data series. Or you may delete some of the data points in a range that is plotted. If you delete data from a range, the chart displays the deleted data as zero values.

To update the chart to reflect the new data range, follow these steps:

1. Activate the chart.

2. Choose the <u>C</u>hart⇨<u>S</u>ource Data command.

3. In the Source Data dialog box, select the tab labeled Series.

4. Select the data series that you want to modify from the list labeled <u>S</u>eries.

5. Use the range selection boxes to change the data series. You may also need to modify the range used for the Category values.

6. Click OK, and the chart is updated with the new data range.

In Step 4, you could select the Data Range tab of the Source Data dialog box and specify the data range for the entire chart.

When you activate a chart, the ranges used by the chart are outlined in the worksheet. To extend or reduce the range, simply drag the handle on the outline in the worksheet.

A better way to handle data ranges that change is to use named ranges. Simply create names for the data ranges that you use in the chart. Activate the chart, select the data series, and edit the SERIES formula by clicking the formula bar. Replace each range reference with the corresponding range name. If you change the definition for a name, the chart is updated.

Changing a chart's scale

Adjusting the scale of a value axis can have a dramatic effect on the appearance of the chart. Excel always determines the scale for your charts automatically. You can, however, override the choice Excel makes:

1. Activate the chart.

2. Select the value (Y) axis.

3. Choose the Format⇨Selected Axis command (or double-click the axis).

4. In the Format Axis dialog box, click the Scale tab.

5. Make the changes and then click OK.

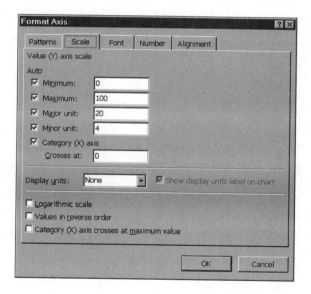

Remember: The dialog box varies slightly depending on which axis is selected.

The Scale tab of the Format Axis dialog box offers the following options:

Minimum: Lets you enter a minimum value for the axis. If checked, Excel determines this value automatically.

Maximum: Lets you enter a maximum value for the axis. If checked, Excel determines this value automatically.

Major unit: Lets you enter the number of units between major tick marks. If checked, Excel determines this value automatically.

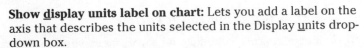

Minor unit: Lets you enter the number of units between minor tick marks. If checked, Excel determines this value automatically.

***Axis Type* axis Crosses at:** Lets you position the axes at a different location. By default, the axes are positioned at the edge of the plot area. The exact wording of this option varies, depending on which axis you select.

Display units: Lets you set the display units for large numbers on the axis. Using this option can make numbers displayed on the axis shorter and more readable.

Show display units label on chart: Lets you add a label on the axis that describes the units selected in the Display units drop-down box.

Logarithmic scale: Lets you use a logarithmic scale for the axes. Useful for scientific applications in which the values to be plotted have an extremely large range; a log scale gives you an error message if the scale includes 0 or negative values.

Values in reverse order: Makes the scale values extend in the opposite direction.

***Axis Type* crosses at maximum value:** Lets you position the axes at the maximum value of the perpendicular axis (normally, the axis is positioned at the minimum value). The exact wording varies, depending on which axis you select.

Changing a chart's gridlines

Gridlines can help you determine what the chart series represents numerically. Gridlines simply extend the tick marks on the axes.

To add or remove gridlines, follow these steps:

1. Activate the chart.

2. Choose the Chart⇨Chart Options command.

3. Click the Gridlines tab.

4. Check or uncheck the check boxes that correspond to the desired gridlines.

Remember: Each axis has two sets of gridlines: major and minor. Major units are the ones displaying a label. Minor units are those in between. If you're working with a 3-D chart, the dialog box has options for three sets of gridlines.

To modify the properties of a set of gridlines, follow these steps:

1. Activate the chart.

2. Select one gridline in the set.

3. Choose the Format➪Selected Gridlines command (or double-click a gridline).

4. In the Format Gridlines dialog box, select the Patterns tab to change the line style, width, and color.

5. In the Format Gridlines dialog box, select the Scale tab to make adjustments to the scale used on the axis, and then click OK.

See also "Changing a chart's scale," in this part.

Changing a chart's location

If your chart is embedded on a worksheet, you can click a border and drag it to a new location on the worksheet. To move the embedded chart to a different sheet or to a separate chart sheet, select the chart and choose the Chart➪Location command. Specify the new location and click OK.

Changing data markers

Excel lets you control various properties of data markers such as size, style, and color.

1. Activate the chart (line chart or XY chart only) and double-click a marker.

   Excel displays the Format Data Series dialog box.

2. Select the Patterns tab.

3. In the Marker section, make your changes.

4. Click OK to close the dialog box.

You can also use a graphic object (such as one of the Excel AutoShapes) for the data markers. Copy the graphic to the Clipboard. Then select a marker in the chart and choose the Edit➪Paste command. You may need to experiment with various sizes.

Changing the chart type

Excel supports a wide variety of chart types (line charts, column charts, and so on).

To change the chart type, follow these steps:

1. Activate the chart.

2. Select the Chart➪Chart Type command to display the Chart Type dialog box.

3. Click the desired chart type.

You can select from standard chart types (in the Standard tab) or custom chart types (listed in the Custom tab). You see a preview of how your chart will look.

4. When you're satisfied with the chart's appearance, click OK.

The chart types displayed in the Custom tab of the Chart Type dialog box are standard chart types that have been modified in one or more ways. Excel comes with a variety of custom chart types, and you can create your own.

Another way to change the chart type is to use the Chart Type tool on the Chart toolbar. This tool displays the major chart types. (You cannot select custom chart types.)

If you've customized some aspects of your chart, choosing a new chart type may override some or all of the changes you've made. For example, if you add gridlines to the chart and then select a chart type that doesn't use gridlines, your gridlines disappear.

See also "Creating a custom chart type," in this part.

Changing the default chart type

Excel's default chart type is a 2-D column chart. If you normally create a different type of chart, you can change the default chart type to your preferred type. To do so, follow these steps:

1. Activate a chart.

2. Choose the Chart⇨Chart Type command.

3. Click the Standard Types tab in the Chart Type dialog box.

4. Select the chart type that you want to use as the default.

5. Click the Set as default chart button and then click OK.

You are asked to confirm this choice.

You can also use a custom chart type as the default. In Step 3, click the Custom Types tab.

If you have many charts of the same type to create, it's much more efficient to change the default chart format to the chart type with which you're working.

Creating a custom chart type

Excel has quite a few custom chart types, and you can create your own user-defined chart type. A custom chart type that you create can be applied to any other chart:

1. Create a chart that's customized the way you want.

For example, you can set any of the colors or line styles, change the scales, modify fonts and type sizes, add gridlines, add a title, and even add free-floating text or graphic images.

2. Activate the chart and choose the Chart⇨Chart Type command.

3. In the Chart Type dialog box click the Custom Types tab.

4. Click the User-defined option.

5. Click the Add button to add a new custom chart type based on the current chart.

Another dialog box appears.

6. In the Add Custom Chart Type dialog box, type a name for the chart type in the top text box and a description in the bottom text box.

7. Click OK to return to the Chart Type dialog box, and then click OK again to return to your chart.

The custom chart type name that you supplied now appears in the Custom Types tab of the Chart Type dialog box. Note that you must click the User-defined option for user-defined chart types to appear.

Creating a default chart on a chart sheet

To quickly create a chart on a new chart sheet, follow these steps:

1. Select the worksheet data to be charted.

2. Press F11.

Excel inserts a new chart sheet and displays the chart based on the selected data. Excel created its default chart type using the default settings.

Remember: For more control over the chart-making process, use the Chart Wizard.

See also "Using the Chart Wizard," in this part.

Deleting a chart element or data series

You can delete any element in a chart.

To delete a chart element, follow these steps:

1. Select the element or data series to be deleted.

2. Press Delete.

See also "Selecting a chart element," in this part.

Remember: If you delete the last data series in a chart, the chart will be empty.

Displaying a data table in a chart

In Excel, you can display a table of the data that's used in the chart. The data table appears below the chart. If you create the chart with the Chart Wizard, you have the opportunity to add the data table in Step 3. To add a data table to an existing chart, follow these steps:

1. Activate the chart.

2. Select the Chart⇨Chart Options command.

Excel displays its Chart Options dialog box.

3. Click the Data Table tab.

4. Click the Show data table checkbox.

5. Depending on your preference for displaying legend keys on the data table, check or clear the check box labeled Show legend keys.

6. Click OK.

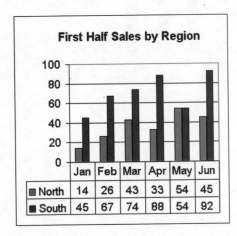

To change the line color or font for the data table, double-click the table and make the changes in the Format Data Table dialog box.

Displaying data labels in a chart

Sometimes, you want your chart to display the actual data values for each point on the chart. Or you may want to display the category label for each data point.

To add data labels to a chart series, follow these steps:

1. Activate the chart.

2. Select the data series.

3. Choose the Format⇨Selected Data Series command (or double-click the data series in the chart).

4. In the Format Data Series dialog box, click the Data Labels tab.

5. Select the option that corresponds to the type of data labels that you want.

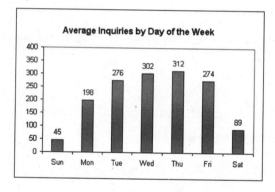

Remember: The data labels are linked to the worksheet, so if your data changes, the labels also change. If you want to override the data label with some other text, select the label and enter the new text (or even a cell reference) in the formula bar.

If the data labels aren't positioned properly, you can select an individual label and move it to a better location by dragging it.

Remember: It is not possible to specify a range of text to be used as data labels. Data labels can consist of either data values or category labels. You must add data labels and then edit each one manually.

Handling missing data in a chart

Sometimes, data that you're charting may be missing one or more data points. Excel offers several options for handling the missing data:

1. Activate the chart.

2. Choose the Tools⇨Options command.

3. In the Options dialog box, click the Chart tab.

4. Select the option that corresponds to how you want to handle the missing data.

The options are as follows:

- **Not plotted (leave gaps):** Missing data is simply ignored, and the data series has a gap for each missing data point.

- **Zero:** Missing data is treated as zero.

- **Interpolated:** Missing data is calculated using data on either side of the missing point(s).

Remember: The options that you set apply to the entire active chart; you can't set a different option for different series in the same chart.

Modifying a chart element

Most elements in a chart can be modified in several ways. For example, you can change colors, line widths, fonts, and so on. Modifications are made in the Format dialog box (which varies for each type of chart element).

To modify an element in a chart, follow these steps:

1. Select the chart element.

2. Access the Format dialog box using any of the following techniques:

- Double-click the item.

- Choose the Format [*Item Name*] command.

- Press Ctrl+1.

- Right-click the item and choose Format [*Item Name*] from the shortcut menu.

3. Click the tab that corresponds to what you want to do.

4. Make the changes.

5. Click OK.

See also "Selecting a chart element," in this part.

Moving a chart element

Some of the chart parts can be moved (any of the titles, data labels, and the legend). To move a chart element, follow these steps:

1. Select the chart element that you want to move.

2. Click the border of the element and drag it to the desired location in the chart.

See also "Selecting a chart element," in this part.

Printing charts

There's nothing special about printing embedded charts; it works just like printing a worksheet. As long as the embedded chart is included in the range to be printed, the chart prints as it appears on-screen.

Remember: If you print in Draft mode, embedded charts don't print.

If you don't want a particular embedded chart to appear on your printout, then just follow these steps:

1. Right-click the chart.

2. Choose Format Chart Area from the Shortcut menu.

3. Activate the Properties tab in the Format Object dialog box.

4. Remove the check mark from the Print object check box.

5. Click OK to close the dialog box.

If the chart is on a chart sheet, it prints on a page by itself. If you access the Excel Page Setup dialog box when the chart sheet is active, you find that the Sheet tab is replaced with a tab named Chart.

The Chart tab has several options:

Use full page: The chart prints to the full width and height of the page margins. Use full page is usually not a good choice because the chart's relative proportions will change and you lose the WYSIWYG (what-you-see-is-what-you-get) advantage.

Scale to fit page: This option expands the chart proportionally in both dimensions until one dimension fills the space between the margins. This option usually results in the best printout.

Custom: This option prints the chart as it appears on your screen. Use the View⇨Sized with Window command to make the chart correspond to the window size and proportions. The chart prints at the current window size and proportions.

Choosing the Print in black and white option prints the data series with black and white patterns rather than colors. This is useful if you don't have a color printer.

Rotating 3-D charts

When you work with 3-D charts, you may find that some data is completely or partially obscured. You can rotate the chart so that it shows the data better:

1. Activate the 3-D chart.

2. Choose the Chart⇨3-D View command.

3. In the 3-D View dialog box, make your rotations and perspective changes by clicking the appropriate controls.

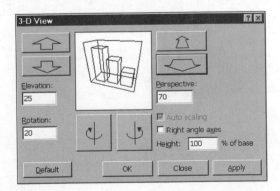

4. Click OK (or click <u>A</u>pply to see the changes without closing the dialog box).

You can also rotate the chart in real time by dragging corners with the mouse. Normally, this procedure displays an outline of the chart's borders only. If you press Ctrl while dragging a corner, you can also see outlines of the chart series.

Selecting a chart element

Modifying an element in a chart is similar to everything else you do in Excel: First you make a selection (in this case, select a chart part), and then you issue a command to do something with the selection.

After you activate a chart, you can select a chart element in any of three ways:

✦ Click the chart element.

✦ Press the up-arrow or down-arrow key to cycle through all the elements in the chart. When a data series is selected, you can press the right-arrow or left-arrow key to select individual points in the series.

✦ Use the Chart Objects control in the Chart toolbar. This is a drop-down list that contains all the elements in the chart.

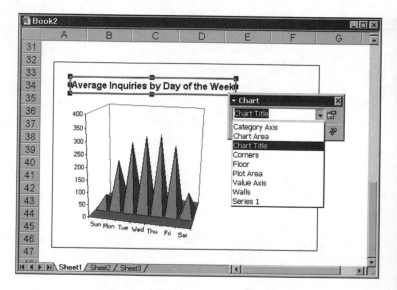

No matter which method you use, the name of the selected item appears in the Name box (at the left of the formula bar). Many of the chart element names include a number that further describes the element. For example, the third point of the first data series is named Series 1 Point 3. You cannot change the names of chart elements, and you cannot select more than one element at a time.

When you move the mouse pointer over a chart element, a chart tip displays the name of the element. If the element is a data point, the chart tip displays the value. To control what appears in these chart tips, use the Tools⇨Options command and click the Chart tab. Make your selection in the Chart tips section of the dialog box.

Using the Chart Wizard

The Chart Wizard consists of a series of four dialog boxes that prompt you for various settings for the chart. By the time you reach the last dialog box, the chart will usually be exactly what you need:

1. Before you invoke the Chart Wizard, you should select the data that you want to include in the chart. Include in your selection items such as labels and series identifiers.

The data that you're plotting doesn't have to be contiguous. You can press Ctrl while making a multiple selection.

2. After selecting the data, invoke the Chart Wizard by clicking the Chart Wizard button on the Standard toolbar. Or you can select the Insert⇨Chart command.

Excel displays the first Chart Wizard dialog box.

Remember: While using the Chart Wizard, you can go back to the previous step by clicking the Back button. Or you can click Finish to end the Chart Wizard. If you end it early, Excel creates the chart using the information you provided up to that point.

Chart Wizard Step 1 of 4

The first step of the Chart Wizard involves selecting the chart type.

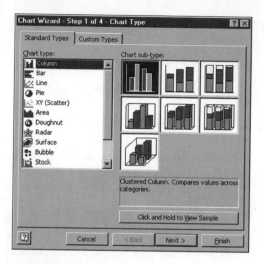

1. Select the chart type.

To use a standard chart type, make your selection in the Standard Types tab. Then choose one of the chart subtypes.

To get a preview of how your data will look with the selected chart type, use the button below the list of chart subtypes. Click the button, but don't release it.

To use a custom chart type, make your selection in the Custom Types tab.

2. Click the Next button to move on to the next step.

Chart Wizard Step 2 of 4

In the second step of the Chart Wizard, you verify (or change) the ranges used in the chart.

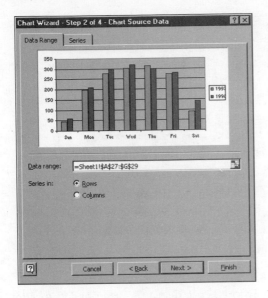

1. Make sure the range displayed in the Data range box is the range that you want to use for the chart.

2. If the data series are in rows, click the Rows option. If the data series are in columns, select the Columns option.

The dialog box displays a preview.

3. If you want to adjust the ranges used for an individual series, click the Series tab and make the changes.

4. Click the Next button to move on to the next step.

Remember: The Row or Column selection in Step 2 is an important choice that has a drastic effect on the look of your chart. Most of the time, Excel guesses the data orientation correctly — but not always.

Chart Wizard Step 3 of 4

The third Chart Wizard dialog box consists of six tabs. Use these tabs to adjust various options for the chart. As you make your selections, the preview chart reflects your choices.

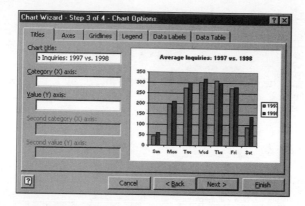

Titles: Enter titles for various parts of the chart.

Axes: Select the type of values to display on the axes.

Gridlines: Specify gridlines, if any.

Legend: Specify whether to display a legend, and its location in the chart.

Data Labels: Specify whether to display data labels (and which type) for the data series.

Data Table: Specify whether to display a table of values used by the chart.

Click Next to move to the final step.

Chart Wizard Step 4 of 4

In Step 4 of the Chart Wizard, you specify where you want the chart to display. You can display it as a new chart sheet or as an object in an existing worksheet (you can select the sheet).

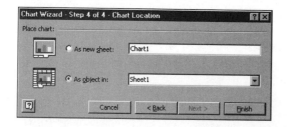

When you click Finish, Excel creates the chart per your specifications.

Remember: You can always change any aspect of the chart by using the procedures described elsewhere in this part. Or you can activate the chart and click the Chart Wizard button to modify an existing chart.

Working with chart legends

If you created your chart with the Chart Wizard, you had an option to include a legend (Step 3). If you change your mind, you can easily delete the legend or add one if you need one.

If you didn't include legend text when you originally selected the cells to create the chart, Excel displays *Series 1, Series 2,* and so on in the legend. To add series names, follow these steps:

1. Activate the chart.

2. Choose the Chart⇨Source Data command.

3. In the Source Data dialog box, click the Series tab.

4. Select a series in the Series box and then enter a name in the Name box. For the name, you can use text or a reference to a cell that contains the series name.

5. Repeat Step 4 for each series that you want to name.

6. Click OK and the new names appear in the legend.

Drawing

In Excel, you find lots of tools, shapes, and formatting options that help you utilize and control the attributes of drawing objects.

Adding a drawing object to a worksheet

Although you can access the drawing tools from the Insert⇨ Picture menu, it's best to display the Drawing toolbar — which contains quick access to all of the drawing features. To display the Drawing toolbar, right-click any toolbar or menu and select Drawing.

The AutoShapes tool expands to show 139 different drawing objects in seven standard categories:

✦ Lines (6 styles)

✦ Connectors (9 styles)

✦ Basic shapes (32 styles)

✦ Block Arrows (28 styles)

✦ Flowchart (28 styles)

✦ Stars and Banners (16 styles)

✦ Callouts (20 styles)

Excel 2000 adds a new drawing object category to the list labeled More AutoShapes. Selecting the More AutoShapes category displays the More Autoshapes dialog box. The dialog box displays a thumbnail list of AutoShapes that have been installed during Microsoft Office 2000 setup and any new shapes that you subsequently add. The More AutoShapes category therefore allows you to build a library consisting of an infinite number of AutoShapes.

Drawing objects with these drawing tools is quite intuitive:

1. Click the AutoShapes tool and select a category.

2. Choose a particular shape from the list that appears.

3. Drag in the worksheet to create the shape (the mouse pointer changes shape, reminding you that you're drawing an object).

4. Release the mouse button.

> The object is drawn and selected, and its name appears in the Name box.

You can control how objects appear with the View tab of the Options dialog box (choose the Tools⇨Options command and select the View tab). Normally, the Show all option is selected. You can hide all objects by choosing Hide all or display objects as placeholders by selecting Show placeholders (this may speed things up if you have complex objects that take a long time to redraw).

✦ To draw an object that has the same height and width dimensions, press Shift while you draw the objects.

✦ To constrain a line or arrow object to angles that are divisible by 15 degrees, press Shift while you draw the object.

✦ To make an object line up precisely to the worksheet row and column gridlines, press the Alt key while you draw the object.

Remember: By default, drawing objects are printed along with the worksheet. If you don't want the objects to print, you have two options:

✦ Access the Sheet panel of the Page Setup dialog box and select the Draft quality option.

✦ Right-click the object, select Format Object from the shortcut menu, and uncheck the Print object check box in the Properties panel.

Adding a shadow to a drawing object

To add a shadow to a drawing object, follow these steps:

1. Select the object.

2. Click the Shadow tool on the Drawing toolbar.

The tool expands to show 20 options.

3. Select one of the shadow options.

Use the tools on the Shadow Settings toolbar to make adjustments.

See also "Making a drawing object three dimensional," in this part.

Aligning drawing objects

If you have several drawing objects on a worksheet, you may want to align them in some way. The easiest way to do this is to let Excel do it for you.

1. Select the objects that you want to align.

2. Click the Draw tool on the Drawing toolbar.

This tool displays a menu.

3. Select Align or Distribute and then one of the Align options in the submenu.

See also "Selecting a group of drawing objects" and "Spacing drawing objects," both in this part.

Changing the stack order of drawn objects

As you add drawing objects to the draw layer of a worksheet, you'll find that objects are stacked on top of each other in the order in which you add them. New objects are stacked on top of older objects.

If you find that an object is obscuring part of another, you can change the order in this stack:

1. Right-click the object to display its shortcut menu.

2. Select the Order⇨Bring to Front command to move the object to the top of the stack. Or select Order⇨Bring Forward to bring the object one step toward the top in the stack order.

3. Select the Order⇨Send to Back command to move the object to the bottom of the stack. Or select Order⇨Send Backward to send the object one step to the bottom in the stack order.

Controlling how objects interact with cells

Objects placed on the draw layer of a worksheet can be moved, resized, copied, and deleted — with no effect on any other elements in the worksheet.

Objects on the draw layer have properties that relate to how they are moved and sized when underlying cells are moved and sized. To change an object's properties, follow these steps:

1. Double-click the object to display its particular Format dialog box.

2. Click the Properties tab in the Format dialog box.

3. Select the appropriate option (as described in the following list) and click OK.

- **Move and size with cells:** If selected, the object appears to be attached to the cells beneath it. For example, if you insert rows above the object, the object moves down. If you increase the column width, the object gets wider.

- **Move but don't size with cells:** If selected, the object moves if rows or columns are inserted, but it never changes its size if you change row heights or column widths.

- **Don't move or size with cells:** If selected, the object will be completely independent of the underlying cells.

Excel also enables you to *attach* an object to a cell. To do so, follow these steps:

1. Choose the Tools⇨Options command.

2. Click the Edit tab of the Options dialog box.

3. Place a check mark next to the check box labeled Cut, copy, and sort objects with cells.

Graphic objects on the draw layer will be attached to the underlying cells.

Copying a drawing object

The easiest way to make an exact copy of a drawing object is to select the object, press Ctrl, and then drag. When you release the mouse button, Excel creates a new copy of the object.

Deleting all drawing objects

To delete all objects on a worksheet, follow these steps:

1. Choose the Edit⇨Go To command (or press F5).

2. Click the Special button in the Go To dialog box.

3. Choose the Objects option button and click OK.

All objects will be selected; press Delete to delete them all.

Grouping and ungrouping objects

Excel lets you combine two or more drawn objects into a single object. This is known as *grouping*. You can manipulate a group as a single object (move it, resize it, and so on).

To group two or more objects, follow these steps:

1. Select all objects that you want in the group by pressing Shift as you click each object.

2. Right-click to display the shortcut menu.

3. Select the Grouping⇨Group command.

If you need to modify one of the objects in the group, you can ungroup them:

1. Right-click the grouped object to display the shortcut menu.

2. Select the Grouping⇨Ungroup command.

Excel breaks the object into its original components.

Making a drawing object three dimensional

To add a 3-D appearance to a drawing object, follow these steps:

1. Select the object.

 2. Click the 3-D tool on the Drawing toolbar.

The tool expands to show 20 options.

3. Select one of the 3-D options.

Use the tools on the 3-D Settings toolbar to make adjustments.

See also "Adding a shadow to a drawing object," in this part.

Modifying drawing objects

After you've drawn an object, you can modify it at any time:

1. Double-click the object to display its Format dialog box.

2. Select the appropriate tab.

3. Make your changes and click OK.

Excel provides lots of formatting options. Formatting changes occur in the Colors and Lines tab. You have a great deal of control over the fill color and fill effects. You can also make an object semi-transparent so the underlying information shows through.

The Drawing toolbar has other tools that let you quickly change the formatting of drawing objects. Feel free to play around with them.

 The various formatting options allow you to modify the characteristics of a given AutoShape object. If you wish to change the AutoShape associated with a given object, select the Draw⇨ Change AutoShape command from the Drawing toolbar.

Moving and resizing drawing objects

To move a drawn object, follow these steps:

1. Click the object to select it.

2. Drag the object to its desired location.

 If you press Alt while moving an object, the object's upper-left corner becomes perfectly aligned to the row and column gridlines.

To move a drawing object one pixel at a time, use the Draw tool on the Drawing toolbar. Clicking this tool displays a menu. Select the Nudge command, and then choose one of the options on the submenu.

To change the size or proportions of a drawn object, follow these steps:

1. Select the object by clicking it once.

2. Click one of its eight *handles.*

The handles are identified by the small squares around the border of the object.

3. Drag until the object reaches the desired size.

To maintain an object's original proportions when you resize the object, press Shift while dragging any of its borders.

Rotating a drawing object

Drawing objects can be rotated to any angle. To rotate a drawing object, follow these steps

1. Select the object.

2. Click the Free Rotate tool on the Drawing toolbar.

The object displays four green handles on its corners.

3. Click and drag one of the handles to rotate the object to the desired angle.

Selecting a group of drawing objects

To select more than one drawing object, you can press Shift as you click the objects that you want to select.

Another way to select a group of objects is to click the Select Objects tool on the Drawing toolbar. After doing so, the mouse pointer turns into an arrow. You can then click and drag to "lasso" a group of drawing objects. To restore the mouse pointer to normal, press Esc (this action will also deselect the objects) or click the Select Objects tool again (this action will not deselect the objects).

Spacing drawing objects

If you have several drawing objects on a worksheet, you can make them evenly spaced.

1. Select the objects that you want to adjust.

2. Click the D<u>r</u>aw tool on the Drawing toolbar.

Clicking this tool displays a menu.

3. Select the Align or Distribute command and then (in the submenu) select Distribute Horizontally or Distribute Vertically.

See also "Selecting a group of drawing objects" and "Aligning drawing objects," both in this part.

Using graphic files

A wide assortment of graphic files (sometimes known as electronic clip art) is available, and you can use these images in your work without violating any copyright restrictions. Excel can import most graphics files that can be placed on a worksheet's draw layer.

To add a graphic file to a worksheet, you can use either of the following options:

✦ Choose the Insert⇨Picture⇨From File command to locate a particular file stored on disk.

✦ Choose the Insert⇨Picture⇨Clip Art command to use the Microsoft Gallery of clip art.

After an image is placed on a worksheet, you can move and resize it. You can also use the tools on the Picture toolbar to manipulate the image. The Picture toolbar appears when you select a picture.

Remember: Depending on the type of image, resizing may or may not produce good results.

Using graphics in a worksheet can dramatically increase the size of your workbook, resulting in more memory usage and longer load and save times.

See also "Applying a background graphic," in Part III.

Web Publishing

Web publishing is the process of placing your Excel data on a Web or intranet server as a Web page. In this process, your Excel data is saved in HTML format. Because your data is in HTML format, users can view your data using their Internet browsers. Excel 97 provided some rudimentary publishing features that were often cumbersome to use. Excel 2000 provides several new features designed to make the publishing process relatively painless.

In Excel 2000, you can publish your data in static or interactive form. If you publish your data in static form, users can only view the data. If you publish your data with interactive functionality, users can work with and manipulate the data within their browsers. Excel 2000 provides three types of interactive functionality:

✦ **Spreadsheet functionality:** When you publish your data with spreadsheet functionality, users can enter and calculate data, format, sort, filter, or cut and paste data in the published sheet.

✦ **PivotTable functionality:** When you publish your data with PivotTable functionality, users can change the layout of a pivot table, format, sort, filter, or cut and paste data in the published pivot table.

✦ **Chart functionality:** When you publish your data with Chart functionality, users can make changes to the source data (which is published with the chart) that will automatically update the chart.

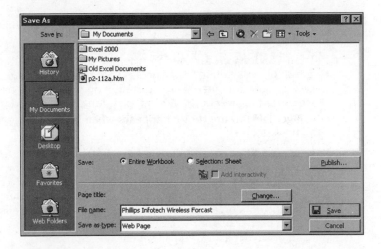

Customizing the way Excel saves a file for publishing

Excel 2000 applies default formatting options when saving a file in HTML format. Excel also gives you the ability to modify many of these options. To customize the way that Excel writes an HTML file, follow these steps:

1. Select the Tools➪Options command and then click the General tab in the Options dialog box.

2. Click the Web Options button.

The last action displays the Web Options dialog box. You can modify the default formatting option settings in any one of the five tabs provided.

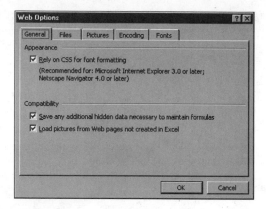

The following describes the options under the Web Options dialog box tabs.

Rely on CSS for font formatting: You find this option under the **General** tab. Cascading Style Sheets (CSS) is a mechanism that describes how documents are presented on screen or in print. Most current browsers provide support for CSS. If you want to accommodate older Web browsers that do not support CSS, clear this check box.

Save any additional hidden data necessary to maintain formulas: You find this option under the **General** tab. If the data on your worksheet begins in a cell other than the upper-left cell (A1), Excel automatically moves your beginning cell of data into cell A1, when you put the data on a Web page. If you want the empty cells in the upper-left corner of your worksheet to appear blank when you publish or save it as a Web page, clear this check box.

Load pictures from Web pages not created in Excel: You find this option under the **General** tab. In general, select this check box if you want to load graphics from a Web page not created in Excel when you open the Web page in Excel 2000. In particular, if you want to use Web queries created by Excel 97 in Excel 2000, you should clear this check box to avoid possible errors in your worksheet that imported pictures displacing data and formulas can cause. Web queries allow you to set up criteria for importing current data from the Internet or an intranet.

Organize supporting files in a folder: You find this option under the **Files** tab. When you save a Web page, Excel by default stores all supporting files — such as bullets, background textures, and graphics — in a separate subfolder. If you want to save supporting files in the same folder as the Web page, clear this check box.

Use long file names whenever possible: You find this option under the **Files** tab. If you use a long file name to save a Web page to a file server, users with Microsoft Windows 3.1 won't be able to find or open your Web page. To always save files for Web pages with short file names, clear this check box.

Update links on save: You find this option under the **Files** tab. If you move or copy your Web page to a new location without moving the supporting files, the links to graphics — such as photos, bullets, and background textures — may be broken. Select this check box to automatically update the paths to all links when you save Web pages in Excel 2000.

Check if Office is the default editor for Web pages created in Office: You find this option under the **Files** tab. Many Web browsers have a setting that specifies which program to use to edit the current Web page (for example, Word or Notepad). For best results, use the program that you created the Web page in to edit the Web page. Select this check box to override the browser's setting so that the browser will use Excel 2000 to edit pages that were created in Excel 2000.

Download Office Web Components: You find this option under the **Files** tab. To create or use Excel 2000 interactive data on the Web, you must install the Web Components that come with Microsoft Office 2000 Professional or Premium Edition. If you have problems using the interactive features on a Web page after you initially install the Web Components, select this check box. In the Location box, type the path for the server or drive letter for the CD-ROM that contains the installation program for Office 2000.

Rely on VML for displaying graphics in browsers: You find this option under the **Pictures** tab. Check this box if you want your Web pages to download faster. To view graphics in Vector Markup Language (VML) format, you must use a browser that supports PNG format, such as Microsoft Internet Explorer 5.0 or later versions.

Allow PNG as an output format: You find this option under the **Pictures** tab. Check this box if you want your workbook to be saved faster, take up less disk space, and download faster. To view graphics in Portable Network Graphics (PNG) format, you must use a browser that supports PNG format, such as Microsoft Internet Explorer 5.0 or later versions.

Target monitor: You find this option under the **Pictures** tab. The screen size you specify for your Web page video resolution can affect the size and layout of images and text on your Web page. Use the Target monitor controls to change the screen and pixel settings to accommodate the intended viewers of your Web page.

Reload the current document as: You find this option under the **Encoding** tab. When you open a Web page that is encoded for a language different from the default language, Excel 2000 tries to determine the language. If Excel displays the wrong characters for that language when you open the page, you can select the language that you think the page is encoded in with the Reload the current document as option.

Save document as: You find this option under the **Encoding** tab. Use this option if you want to specify the language code that Excel should use to save your Web page. This option is mutually exclusive with the Always save Web pages in the default encoding option.

Always save Web pages in the default encoding: You find this option under the **Encoding** tab. Check this check box if you want Excel to always save your Web pages using the default language encoding. This option is mutually exclusive with the Save document as option.

Character Set, Proportional font, Fixed-width font: You find these options under the **Fonts** tab. If the wrong character set or font for a Web page or plain text file is applied when you import a Web page into Excel 2000, the Web page may not display correctly. This option enables you to select the character set and font that you think the page is encoded in. Proportional font is used for normal text. Fixed-width font is used for monospace text.

Remember: Most of the Web Option settings apply to the current page and any future pages that you save in Excel 2000.

See also "Publishing your worksheet data to a Web page," in this part.

Publishing your worksheet data to a Web page

To publish worksheet data to a Web page, follow these steps:

1. Select the worksheet that contains the data that you want to put on a Web page.

2. Select the File➪Save as Web Page command.

3. In the Save As dialog box, click the Publish button.

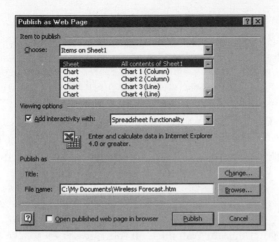

4. In the Publish as Web Page dialog box, make a selection from the Choose list box. This list box provides three main selections:

- **Previously published items:** Use this option to republish your data. See the next section, Republishing your worksheet data to the Web, for use of this option.

- **Range of cells:** Use this option to publish a range of cells on your worksheet. This option is automatically selected for you if the range is selected prior to Step 2 of this procedure.

- **Items on *<Sheetname>*:** Use this option to publish items on *<Sheetname>*, where *<Sheetname>* is the actual name of the worksheet on which you want to publish the items. This option is automatically selected if you do not select a specific item on *<Sheetname>* prior to Step 2 of this procedure.

5. In the selection box below the Choose list box, select the range or worksheet item you want to publish.

If you selected Items on *<Sheetname>* in Step 4, the selection box may display up to five items, depending on the objects in your worksheet. These items are: Sheet (for example, all data), Chart, PivotTable, AutoFilter, and Print Area.

6. In the File name box, type the pathname and filename where you want to save your worksheet or worksheet items. Click the Browse button to help you locate the appropriate directory, folder, intranet, or Internet location.

You may also check any or all of the following options prior to Step 7:

- **Add Interactivity with:** Check this box if you want to allow users to manipulate the data after it is published. Select the appropriate functionality (spreadsheet, pivot table, or chart functionality as applicable) from the list box.

- **Change:** Click this button if you want to add a title for the Web page.

- **Open published Web page in browser:** Check this box if you want to view the Web page in your browser after you save or publish it.

7. Click the Publish button.

Before you put your Web page on the Web server where users will view it, it's a good idea to put the Web page on your hard drive or file server so you can confirm that the page appears and is working properly. Another good idea is to check your Web page in different browsers before publishing it to see how the different browsers affect the format of your document.

If you select the sheet, range, chart, pivot table, autofilter, or print area prior to choosing the File➪Save as Web Page command, you can skip the Publish as Web page dialog box by clicking the Selection: *<Item>* radio button in the Save As dialog box. *<Item>* may be Sheet, Chart, PivotTable, AutoFilter, Print Area, or a range of cells. All the options in the Publish as Web page dialog box are available to you, except Open published Web page in a browser.

Remember: If you select a worksheet that contains a chart and save or publish it with spreadsheet functionality, the chart is not included on the Web page.

Remember: You may not be able to view all the formatting options applied to your document when the file is opened in a Web browser, because Excel embeds additional information describing complex formatting options to the HTML file. Many browsers are unable to interpret this additional information.

Republishing your worksheet data to the Web

Republishing data enables you to easily update a Web page that you've already put on the Web using Excel 2000. Republishing allows you to update the Excel data, publish the data to a new location, change whether the data is interactive, and change the title of the data.

To republish your data, follow these steps:

1. Open the Excel workbook file that contains the worksheet items that you previously saved as a Web page and want to update.

2. When you've finished updating your data, select the File⇨Save As Web Page command.

3. In the File Save As dialog box, click the Publish button.

4. In the Publish as Web page dialog box, select Previously published items in the Choose list box.

5. In the selection box below the Choose list box, select the range or worksheet item you wish to publish.

6. If you want to change the interactivity, title, or file location of your document, make the changes in the appropriate dialog boxes.

7. Click the Publish button.

Remember: To republish data using the previous procedure, you must resave your Excel worksheet after each publishing (or republishing) session.

See also "Publishing your worksheet data to a Web page," in this part.

Techie Talk

Absolute reference: In a formula, a reference to a cell that does not change if the formula is copied to a different cell. An absolute reference uses two dollar signs, such as A15 for cell A15.

Active cell: The cell whose contents appear in the formula bar. You can enter information into the active cell and also edit its contents.

Add-in: A file that is loaded into Excel in order to provide additional commands or worksheet functions.

Analysis ToolPak: An add-in that provides Excel with specialized analytical tools and worksheet functions.

Argument: In a worksheet function, information (enclosed in parentheses) that provides details as to what you want the function to do.

Array formula: A special type of formula used by advanced users.

Autofilter: To display only the rows in a list that meet certain criteria.

Autoformat: Predefined formatting that you can quickly apply to a range of cells in a worksheet or a pivot table. Also refers to predefined formats that you can apply to a chart.

AutoShape: A graphic object that you place on the draw layer using one of the Excel drawing tools.

Cell: A single addressable unit in a worksheet, defined by the intersection of a row and a column.

Cell comment: A comment that is attached to a cell.

Cell pointer: The dark border that surrounds the active cell. You move the cell pointer with the mouse or the keyboard.

Cell reference: Identifies a cell by giving its column letter and row number. For example, C5 refers to the cell at the intersection of column C and row 5. If you're referring to a cell on a different sheet, you need to precede it with the sheet name and an exclamation point. These can be relative references (most common), absolute references, or mixed references.

Chart: A graphic representation of values in a worksheet. A chart can be embedded on a worksheet or stored on a separate chart sheet in a workbook.

Chart sheet: A type of sheet in a workbook that holds a single chart.

ChartWizard: A series of interactive dialog boxes that help you create charts.

Check box: In a dialog box, an option that you can turn either on or off (by clicking it). This is not the same as an option button.

Circular reference: In a formula, a reference to the cell that contains the formula (either directly or indirectly). If cell A10 contains =SUM(A1:A10), a circular reference exists because the formula refers to its own cell.

Clipboard: An area of your computer's memory that stores information that has been copied or cut from an application.

Column: Part of a worksheet that consists of 65,536 cells arranged vertically. Each worksheet has 256 columns.

Conditional formatting: Formatting (such as color or bold text) that is applied to a cell depending on the cell's contents.

Consolidation: The process of merging data from multiple worksheets or multiple workbook files.

Criteria range: A special type of range that holds specifications used by an advanced filter or for a database worksheet function.

Data table: A table, calculated by Excel, that shows the effects on one or more formulas when one or more input cells take on different values. Excel supports one-way and two-way data tables.

Data validation: The process of ensuring that data of the correct type is entered into a cell. For example, if the entry is outside of a specified range of values, you can display a message to the user.

Database: A systematic collection of information comprised of records (rows) and fields (columns). A database can be stored in a worksheet (where it's known as a list) or in an external file.

Default workbook template: A template that is used as the basis for new workbooks. This template is named book.xlt and is stored in your XLStart folder.

Default worksheet template: A template that is used as the basis for new worksheets that you insert into a workbook. This template is named sheet.xlt and is stored in your XLStart folder.

Dependent cell: A cell that contains a formula that refers to the active cell. In other words, the formula depends on the value in the active cell.

Dialog box: An interactive window that appears in response to most commands. A dialog box is used to get additional information from you so Excel can carry out the command.

Double-click: To click the left mouse button rapidly twice.

Drag: To hold down the mouse button to move an object or extend a selection of cells.

Drag-and-drop: To use the mouse to grab something, move it, and drop it somewhere else. You can use drag-and-drop to move a cell, a range, or a graphic object.

Draw layer: An invisible layer on top of all worksheets. The draw layer contains embedded charts, maps, and drawn objects.

Drawn object: A graphic object that you place on the draw layer using one of the Excel drawing tools.

Drop-down list box: In a dialog box, a control that normally only shows one option. If you select this control, it drops down a list to show more options.

Embedded chart: A chart that's placed on a worksheet's draw layer (as opposed to residing on a separate chart sheet).

Export: To save information in a file format that can be used by another application.

Field: In a database, information that is contained in columns.

Fill handle: The small square object that appears at the lower-right corner of the active cell or a selected range of cells.

Filter: To hide rows in a list such that only the rows that meet a certain criteria are displayed.

Font: The typeface used for text and values.

Formatting: The process of changing the appearance of a cell, range, or object.

Formula: An entry in a cell that returns a calculated result.

Formula bar: The area of Excel, just below the toolbars, that displays the contents of the active cell. You can edit the cell in the formula bar.

Formula palette: A tool that helps you create and edit formulas and worksheet functions.

Frozen titles: The process of keeping certain top rows and/or left columns always displayed, no matter where the

cell pointer is. You can set this with the Window⇨Freeze Panes command.

Function: A special keyword used in a formula to perform a calculation. Use the Function Wizard to enter a function in a formula.

Functionality: A new feature in Excel 2000 that describes how portions of a worksheet are published interactively to the Web. Spreadsheet functionality allows speadsheet data to be published interactively. PivotTable functionality allows a pivot table to be published interactively. Chart functionality allows a Chart to be published interactively. *See also* Interactive Publishing.

Goal seeking: The process of determining the value of a cell that results in a specific value returned by a formula.

Gridlines: Lines that delineate the cells in a worksheet. In a chart, gridlines are extensions of the tick marks on the axes.

Handles: On graphic objects, these are the small squarish things at the corners and on the sides. You can drag handles with a mouse to change the size of the graphic object.

HTML document: A document formatted for the World Wide Web using special formatting codes.

Hyperlink: A word or phrase (usually underlined) that, when clicked, opens a new document. A graphic can also be a hyperlink.

Icon: A small picture that you can click with your mouse. In this book, a small picture in the left margin that calls your attention to various types of information.

Import: To retrieve information from a file that was saved by another application.

IntelliMouse: The special mouse, manufactured by Microsoft. This mouse is equipped with a small wheel between the two buttons. In Excel, spinning the wheel can scroll the worksheet vertically, or zoom in and out on a worksheet.

Interactive Publishing: A new feature in Excel 2000 that publishes data to a Web page in such a way that you can manipulate the data though a browser. For example, using the Internet Explorer browser, a user can format, sort, or file data in a published spreadsheet or pivot table or make changes to the source data in a published chart that automatically updates the chart.

Legend: In a chart, the small box that describes the data series. In a map, the small box that describes the map's contents.

Link formula: A formula that uses a reference to a cell that's contained in a different workbook.

List: A database that's stored in a worksheet. A list contains a header row that describes the contents of the information in each column.

Locked cell: A cell that cannot be changed when the worksheet is protected. If the worksheet is not protected, locked cells can be modified.

Macro: A miniprogram that automatically executes a series of statements or actions. Macros are used to automate repetitive procedures.

Map: A graphic depiction of data that is based on geography.

Maximize: To make a window as large as it can be.

Menu bar: A special toolbar that contains commands. Normally, the menu bar is located just below the title bar.

Merged cells: Cells that have been combined into one larger cell that holds a single value.

Minimize: To make a window as small as it can be.

Mixed reference: In a formula, a reference to a cell that is partially absolute and partially relative. A mixed reference uses one dollar sign, such as A$15 for cell A15. In this case, the column part of the reference is relative; the row part of the reference is absolute.

Mouse pointer: The object that you see move on-screen when you move your mouse. The mouse pointer often changes its shape, depending on what you're doing at the time.

Named range: A range that you've assigned a name to. Using named ranges in formulas makes your formulas more readable.

Noncontiguous range: A range of cells that is not contained in a single rectangular area. You select a noncontiguous range by pressing Ctrl while you select cells.

Number format: The manner in which a value is displayed. For example, you can format a number to appear with a percent sign and a specific number of decimal places. The number format changes only the appearance of the number (not the number itself).

Office Assistant: A feature in Microsoft Office that provides a variety of interactive help and assistance with various features.

Office Clipboard: A new feature in Microsoft Office 2000 that allows you to copy up to 12 items at a time for pasting into any Office 2000 application. In contrast, with the Windows Clipboard you can only copy one item at a time.

OLE object: An object from another application that is stored in a document. OLE stands for *Object Linking and Embedding.*

Operator: In a formula, a character that represents the type of operation to be performed. Operators include + (plus sign), / (division sign), & (text concatenation), and others.

Option button: In a dialog box, one of a group of buttons. Only one button in the group can be selected at any time. Sometimes called Radio buttons.

Outline: A worksheet structured in such a way that information can be expanded (to show additional details) or contracted (to show fewer details).

Page break: A dashed line that appears on-screen to tell you where the pages will break when you print the worksheet. Page breaks are either natural or can be specified manually.

Page Break Preview mode: An editable view that superimposes page numbers and page breaks on the worksheet. You can drag the page breaks to move them.

Pane: One part of a worksheet window that has been split into either two or four parts.

Paste: To retrieve information that was copied or cut and stored on the Clipboard.

Pivot table: A table that summarizes information contained in a worksheet list or external database.

Pointing: The process of selecting a range using either the keyboard or the mouse. When you need to enter a cell or range reference into a dialog box, you can either enter it directly or point to it in the worksheet.

Precedent cell: A cell that is referred to by a formula cell. A single formula can have many precedent cells, and the precedents can be direct or indirect.

Print titles: One or more rows and/or columns that appear on each page of printed output.

Range: A collection of two or more cells. Specify a range by separating the upper-left cell and the lower-right cell with a colon.

Range Finder: The colored frame that indicates cells that are referenced in a formula or used in a chart. You can grab and move the frame to change the formula or chart series.

Recalculate: To update a worksheet's formulas using the most current values.

Record: In a database, information that is contained in rows.

Redo: To reverse the effects of an Undo operation.

Relative reference: In a formula, a reference to a cell that changes (in a relative manner) if the formula is copied to a different cell. A relative reference doesn't use any dollar signs (as opposed to an absolute reference or a mixed reference).

Restore: To return a window (either the Excel window or a workbook window) to its previous size.

Row: Part of a worksheet that consists of 256 cells arranged horizontally. Each worksheet has 65,536 rows.

Scenario: A specific set of values for input cells. Each scenario is assigned a name and can be displayed using the Excel scenario manager.

Scrap: A range of information that is dragged to the Windows desktop. This scrap can then be dragged into another application.

Scroll bar: One of two bars (on the right and bottom of a workbook window) that let you scroll quickly through the worksheet using the mouse.

Selection: The item that is currently activated. A selection can be a cell or range, a part of a chart, or one or more graphic objects.

Setup: The name of the program that you run to install Excel. Sometimes you need to rerun Setup to add features that were not installed during the original installation.

Sheet: One unit of a workbook, which can be a worksheet or a chart sheet. Activate a sheet by clicking its sheet tab.

Shortcut menu: The context-sensitive menu that appears when you right-click a cell, range, or object.

Sort: To rearrange the order of rows, based on the contents of one or more columns. Sorts can be in ascending or descending order.

Spreadsheet: A generic term for a product such as Excel that is used to track and calculate data. Or, this term is often used to refer to a worksheet or a workbook.

Status bar: The line at the bottom of the Excel window that shows the status of several things and also displays some messages.

Template: A file that is used as the basis for a new workbook. Examples include the Spreadsheet Solutions templates that come with Excel.

Text attributes: Formats that are applied to cell contents. These include bold, underline, italic, and strikethrough.

Text file: A file that contains data only and no formatting. A text file is sometimes referred to as an ASCII file.

Title bar: The colored bar at the top of every window. Drag the title bar with the mouse to move a non-maximized window.

Toolbar: A collection of buttons that serve as shortcuts for common commands.

Undo: To reverse the effects of the last command (or as many as 16 of the previous commands) with the Edit➪Undo command (or Ctrl+Z).

Value: A number entered into a cell.

VBA: Visual Basic for Applications. This is the name of the macro language included with Excel.

What-if analysis: The process of changing one or more input cells and observing the effects on one or more dependent formulas. The Excel Scenario Manager makes it easy to perform what-if analyses.

Window: A container for an application or a workbook. You can move and resize windows.

Wizard: A series of dialog boxes that assist you in performing an operation such as creating a chart, importing text, or creating certain types of formulas.

Workbook: The name for a file that Excel uses. A workbook consists of one or more sheets.

Worksheet: A sheet in a workbook that contains cells. Worksheets are the most commonly used sheet type.

Workspace file: A file that contains information about all open workbooks: their size, arrangement, and position. You can save a workspace file and then re-open it to pick up where you left off.

Zoom: To expand or contract the size of the text displayed in a window. Zoom in to make text larger and zoom out to make text smaller so you can see more.

Index

Numbers

3-D charts, rotating, 171–172
3-D drawing objects,
    creating, 182
3-D tool, 182
3-D View dialog box, 171–172

A

absolute reference, 115–116,
    193
active cell
    defined, 7, 193
    formula bar display, 7
active workbooks, saving, 25
active worksheet
    creating a new view, 32–33
    printing, 74
    multiple panes, 37–38
    zoom factor, 38
Add Trendline dialog box,
    trend types, 158–159
add-in, 193
add-in functions, 119
addresses, 6
Advanced Filter dialog box,
    136–137
advanced filtering, 137
Advanced Text Import
    Settings dialog box,
    import options, 19
Align Center button, 44
Align Left button, 44
Align Right button, 44
Alt key, 13
Analysis ToolPak, 193
animation, Office Assistant,
    9–10
arguments, 118, 193
arithmetic operators,
    formulas, 6
array formula, 193
asterisk (*) character,
    multiplication
    operator, 6
attributes
    named styles, 52
    text, 49
auditing, 128–129
Auditing toolbar, tools,
    129–130

AutoComplete, 98–99
AutoFill
    described, 99–101
    incremental date/value
        series entry, 100
    text entry, 100–101
AutoFill handle, copying a
    cell to another cell or
    range, 79
autofilter, 193
autofiltering
    custom list autofiltering,
        135–136
    described, 134–135
autoformat, 60, 193
AutoFormat dialog box, 42
Automatic Calculation
    mode, 112–113
automatic decimal points,
    101
AutoSave Add-in, 27
AutoShape, 193
AutoShapes tool, 178

B

backgrounds
    cell formatting, 44–45
    hiding cell contents, 56
backups, workbook, 25
Bold tool (Ctrl+B), 49
borders, adding to a cell or
    range, 42–43
buttons
    dialog box element, 12
    toggles, 43

C

Calculated Field dialog box,
    pivot table insertion,
    153–154
Calculation mode, setting,
    112–113
calculations, subtotal
    formulas, 110–112
Cancel button, dialog box
    element, 12
cell comment, 194
cell edit mode
    content editing, 81–83
    enabling, 81
    key combinations, 82–83

cell formatting
    AutoFormat feature, 60
    background colors/
        patterns, 44–45
    background graphics, 45
    border addition, 42–43
    character selection
        methods, 54–55
    column width settings, 47
    conditional formatting, 55
    content alignments, 44
    copying formats between
        cells, 50–51
    custom number formats,
        51–52
    default font (typeface)
        modification, 47
    font sizing, 48
    indents, 57
    justification, 57–58
    methods, 42
    named styles, 46, 52–53
    number formats, 53–54
    right-aligned numbers, 44
    row height settings, 48–49
    style by example, 52
    text attributes, 49
    text colors, 46
    text orientation, 49–50
    wrapping text, 60–61
cell names
    advantages of, 121
    conventions, 121–122
cell pointer, 194
cell references
    applying name to, 122
    defined, 194
    formula element, 85
    remote workbooks,
        114–115
cell tracers, 130
cells
    active, 7
    address conventions, 6
    AutoFill handle, 79
    comments, 101–102
    content editing, 81–83
    copying, 78–81
    copying data as a picture,
        79
    copying to another cell or
        a range, 79

Notes

Notes

Notes

Notes